DEBATE Pro
Book 2

Author Jonathan S. McClelland
- BA in English with a Writing Concentration, University of South Carolina, Columbia, SC, USA
- Former English instructor at Daewon Foreign Language High School
- Current debate instructor for elementary school students
- Former curriculum developer at Korean Army Intelligence School
- Expert test developer of TOEFL, TOEIC, and TEPS

DEBATE Pro Book 2

Publisher Chung Kyudo
Editors Hong Inpyo, Cho Sangik
Proofreader Michael A. Putlack
Designers Zo Hwayoun, Oh Younjoo

First Published in July 2013
By Darakwon, Inc.
Darakwon Bldg., 211, Munbal-ro, Paju-si, Gyeonggi-do 10881
Republic of Korea
Tel: 82-2-736-2031 (Ext. 250)
Fax: 82-2-732-2037

Copyright © 2013 Darakwon, Inc.

All rights reserved. No part of this publication may be reproduced, stored in a retrieval system, or transmitted in any form or by any means, electronic, mechanical, photocopying or otherwise, without the prior consent of the copyright owner. Refund after purchase is possible only according to the company regulations. Contact the above telephone number for any inquiries. Consumer damages caused by loss, damage, etc. can be compensated according to the consumer dispute resolution standards announced by the Korea Fair Trade Commission. An incorrectly collated book will be exchanged.

ISBN 978-89-277-0680-9 58740
         978-89-277-0677-9 58740 (set)

www.darakwon.co.kr

Components Main Book / Workbook
18 17 16 15 14 13 12   25 26 27 28 29

Instilling Knowledge and Skills
for Thoughtful Debate

DEBATE Pro

Book 2

DARAKWON

Preface

The *Debate Pro* series is designed to provide students with an intermediate EFL ability with a sound understanding of a variety of debate topics and develop their speaking, listening, and critical thinking skills through debate. The series consists of eight sets of books, each of which includes a Main Book and a Workbook. Each Main Book includes five chapters covering five debate skills. Within each chapter, there are two units which each cover different topics for a total of ten debate topics per book. The Workbook supplements the Main Book by helping students understand the topic more deeply, developing skills for making examples and doing research, and evaluating the debates. The Workbook can be used in class and for homework assignments.

In the book, every debate topic is introduced with a large color photograph relating to the topic. Students are asked to analyze the picture and formulate opinions about the topic through a series of six warm-up questions. The topic is then explained in more detail through a reading passage of about 300 words which briefly presents background information about the topic before outlining arguments in favor of and against the topic. The passages are followed by vocabulary and comprehension exercises. Students are then required to apply what they have learned from the passage to answer a series of in-depth questions relating to the debate topic. Following these questions, students are given opinion examples before learning the debate skill for each topic. Finally, students will have the chance to apply their knowledge to create a full debate with the assistance of sample arguments and a debate flow chart.

Each book provides free MP3 files with recordings of the reading passages and opinion examples for every unit. There is also a Teacher's Guide available at www.darakwon.co.kr that includes answer keys and sample answers for every unit as well as teaching tips and suggestions for supplementing the material.

The *Debate Pro* series has the following features:

- Ten different debate topics per book covering a range of themes including education, technology, relationships, and responsibility
- Reading passages which provide a general understanding of arguments both for and against the given topic
- Questions that require students to formulate arguments and supporting opinions about each topic
- Five different debate skills per book designed to improve students' critical thinking and speaking skills
- Sample opinions and argument examples which help students develop their own arguments
- Free MP3 files with recordings of all passages and sample opinions

Contents

About This Book _7

Chapter 1
Organizing Supporting Arguments

- **Unit 01** Afterschool Academies _12
- **Unit 02** Genetically Modified Foods _22

Chapter 2
Developing Logical Supporting Reasons

- **Unit 03** Climate Change _34
- **Unit 04** Replacing Teachers with Computers _44

Chapter 3
Developing Effective Supporting Reasons

- **Unit 05** Using CCTVs in Public Places _56
- **Unit 06** Celebrity Salaries _66

Chapter 4
Giving Supporting Examples

- **Unit 07** Punishment for Criminals _78
- **Unit 08** Cosmetic Plastic Surgery _88

Chapter 5
Doing Research

- **Unit 09** Physical Education in Schools _100
- **Unit 10** Space Exploration _110

About This Book

Overview

Debate Pro main book consists of five chapters. Each chapter contains two units with each focusing on the same debate skill. Every unit is further subdivided into part A and part B. Part A, Learning about the Topic, introduces students to the topic of the unit and consists of approximately one hour of learning material. Part B, Debating the Topic, requires students to formulate their arguments and debate the topic of the unit. The total time required for Part B is also approximately one hour.

Introduction for each section

Warm-up

This part includes a picture related to the topic for students to analyze. The pictures are followed by six warm-up questions. The questions in Part A require students to analyze the picture and can be answered as a class. In Part B, students draw upon their knowledge about the topic to answer questions with a partner.

Reading Passage

This part consists of a single reading passage approximately 300 words in length. The passage introduces general background information about the topic and presents specific arguments with examples both in favor of and against the topic.

Vocabulary Check

Each reading passage is followed by five vocabulary questions to bolster students' vocabulary and ensure their understanding of the passage.

Comprehension Questions

Each reading passage includes four paired-choice reading comprehension questions. The questions ask students about the main idea of passage, factual information, and reasoning from the passage.

Questions for Debate

This portion consists of five open-ended questions related to the topic. The students must formulate opinions about each question and give reasons for their opinions. Key phrases are provided to help students improve their speaking skills.

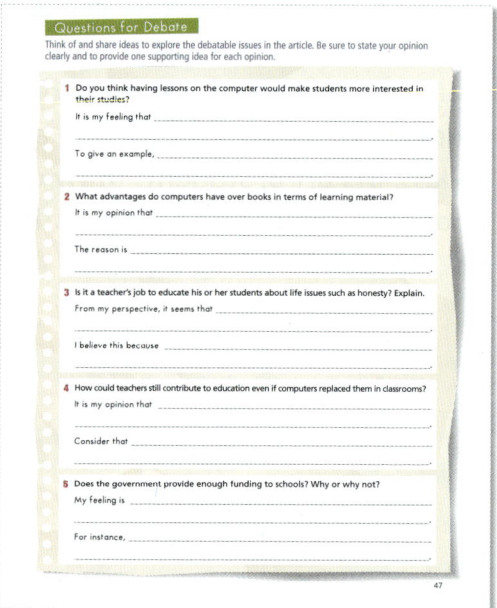

Opinion Examples

In this section, two opinion examples for and against the topic are provided. Students are required to understand the main idea of each example opinion and its supporting arguments. They must also provide an additional argument for each opinion.

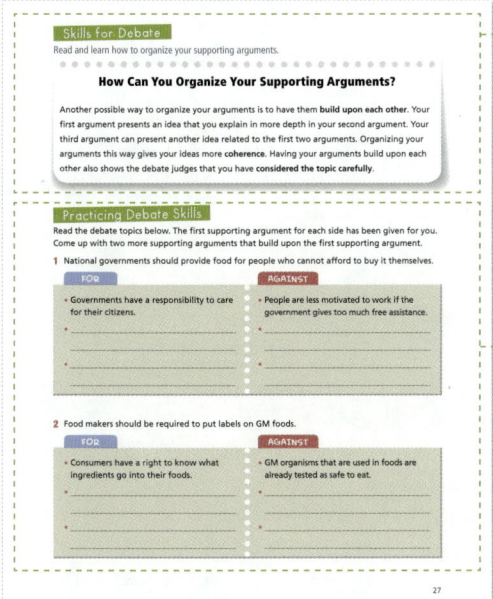

Skills for Debate

This section introduces a debate skill and explains key concepts related to the topic. Each chapter focuses on a single debate skill across two units.

Practicing Debate Skills

This exercise follows each debate skill explanation to ensure that students understand the skill and can use it during their debate.

Creating Your Debate

This section begins by introducing the skills of ARE: Argument, Reason, and Example. Following this are two sample arguments, one for PRO and one for CON, with sample notes for the ARE. On the next page are three blank columns for students to work in teams and create their AREs.

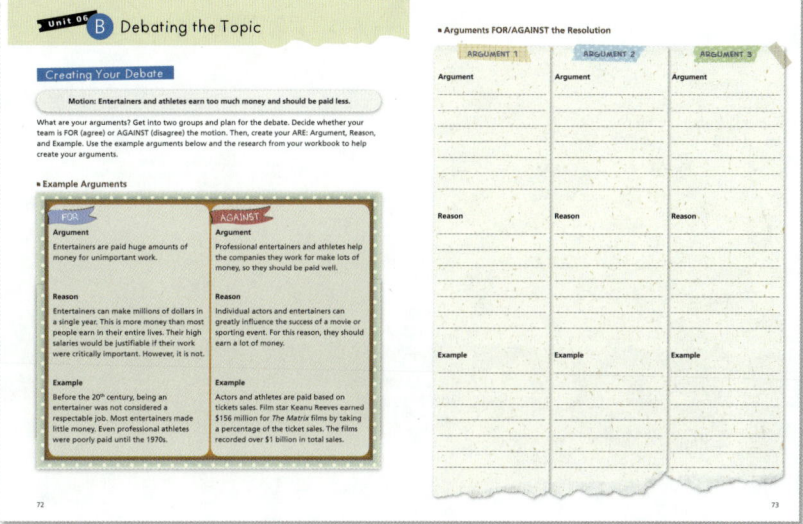

Actual Debate

This portion consists of a debate flow chart. The chart outlines the order of debate and provides sample phrases to help students use proper debate language.

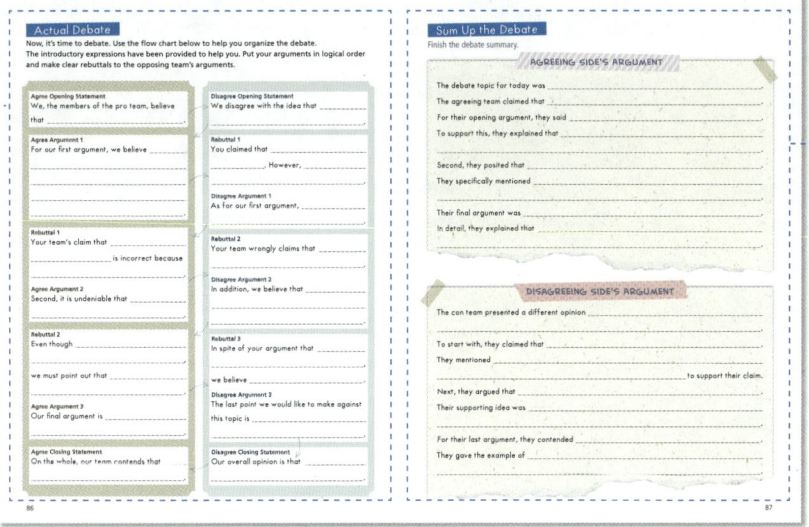

Sum Up the Debate

The final section requires students to summarize the arguments presented by both the PRO and CON teams during the debate. Sample phrases are given to help students.

Chapter 1

Organizing Supporting Arguments

Unit 01 Afterschool Academies

Unit 02 Genetically Modified Foods

Unit 01 Afterschool Academies

WARM-UP

A. Discuss the following questions as a class.
1. What do you see in the picture above?
2. Why do you think the girl is tired? Explain.
3. How do you think afterschool academies have negative effects on students?

B. Answer the following questions with a partner.
1. Do you think afterschool academies help you learn more than you would at school?
2. Why do you think afterschool academies were originally created?
3. What are the main benefits of afterschool academies for students? For nations?

Unit 01 A Learning about the Topic

Should students study at after school academies?

Read the passage and underline the main ideas.

 Track 01

Many nations in East Asia place great value on education. At the same time, the pressure to succeed in these nations is **intense**. This has led millions of parents to send their children to private afterschool academies, which are sometimes called cram schools. Parents and students often believe that going to these academies is necessary for success in life. Even so, many worry that attending academies may put too much pressure on young students.

By studying at afterschool academies, students can develop their academic skills. Academies enable students to get better grades and higher test scores. These can help them be accepted to better colleges and get high-paying jobs. Afterschool academies also help students **pursue** many different academic interests. The most popular academies are ones that teach English, math, and science. However, there are also academies teaching history, musical instruments, and even magic performances. In addition, nations directly benefit from afterschool academies. A more educated workforce means more economic growth. This has been true for South Korea, Taiwan, and other countries. They have relied on their educated workforces to escape **poverty** and to become wealthy.

Nevertheless, not all news is good for academies. Some information suggests that too much studying might harm young people. From as young as the age of four, students begin to feel pressure to succeed. This can lead to serious mental and physical health problems. Likewise, academies leave children little time to play and to have fun. Many childcare experts believe that playing is just as important for young children as classroom learning. It gives them physical exercise and teaches them how to **socialize** with others. Another problem is the high price of academies. A single academy can cost hundreds of dollars a month. Parents often send their children to several different academies. This means that parents have to work extra hours or take out **loans** to pay for the afterschool academies their children attend.

Vocabulary Check

Choose the correct word for each definition.

| intense | pursue | poverty | socialize | loan |

1 to talk and do things with other people in friendly way _____
2 to try to get something over a long time _____
3 the state of being poor _____
4 an amount of money that is borrowed _____
5 very great in degree; very strong _____

Comprehension Questions

Check the correct answer for each question.

1 What do many nations in East Asia place great value on?
- ☐ Education
- ☐ History

2 Which types of academies are the most popular?
- ☐ English, math, and science
- ☐ history, music, and magic

3 Why is it important for young children to play?
- ☐ Because they have more time to review the material they study at school
- ☐ Because they get physical exercise and learn how to socialize with others

4 How do private academies affect parents?
- ☐ They give parents less time to spend socializing with their children.
- ☐ They require parents to work overtime or to borrow money from the bank.

Questions for Debate

Think of and share ideas to explore the debatable issues in the article. Be sure to state your opinion clearly and to provide one supporting idea for each opinion.

1. Would you prefer to go to afterschool academies or to take extra classes at school?

   I would prefer to _____
   _____.

   I feel this way because _____
   _____.

2. Do you believe afterschool academies help children learn more? Why or why not?

   I believe that _____
   _____.

   For instance, _____
   _____.

3. How much playtime do you think children should have each week?

   I think that _____
   _____.

   To give an example, _____
   _____.

4. Do you think some societies such as South Korea have become too competitive? Explain.

   To me, it seems that _____
   _____.

   For example, _____
   _____.

5. Why do you think some government officials try to regulate and even close afterschool academies?

   My reasoning is _____
   _____.

   Consider that _____
   _____.

Opinion Examples

Look at the opinion examples about the motion below and answer the questions.

Motion: Afterschool academies help students and nations become more successful.

Opinion A Track 02

Afterschool academies definitely help students learn more and get better grades. But students also need to spend time outside the classroom. Students who go to afterschool academies can spend up to 12 hours a day studying. That's just too much studying. Children need to play outside. They need to spend time talking with other children and making friends. They also need to exercise. One of my favorite things about living in Canada for a year was being able to play after school each day. I was able to make a lot of friends and to have fun. But I was also able to relax and to get rid of my stress.

Opinion B Track 03

Critics complain that afterschool academies place too much pressure on students. The fact is that afterschool academies are necessary. The world today is a very competitive place. Students need every advantage possible to get ahead. At competitive schools, a difference of only one grade point can mean success or failure. Afterschool academies give students the knowledge they need to get ahead. The bigger picture is that afterschool academies benefit nations. Thanks to these academies, nations can have large, educated workforces. These help countries develop more advanced technology and industries. Nations can become richer as a result.

1 Underline the main idea of each opinion.

2 Which opinion is for the topic? Which one is against it?
- FOR: _____
- AGAINST: _____

3 What supporting ideas does each opinion give?
- Opinion A: _____
- Opinion B: _____

4 Create one more supporting idea for each argument.
- Opinion A: _____
- Opinion B: _____

Skills for Debate

Read and learn how to organize your supporting arguments.

How Can You Organize Your Supporting Arguments?

To win a debate, you must create strong supporting arguments. However, you should not present the arguments in any order you want. You must organize your supporting arguments in **order of importance**. Your first argument should always be your most important argument. An important argument is one that is the most **convincing**, has a strong influence on **society**, or has an **emotional appeal**. Your following arguments are still important but are not as important as your first argument.

Practicing Debate Skills

Read each of the debate topics below and their arguments. Place each of the arguments in order from most important to least important. Put the most important argument first and the least important argument last. Finally, explain why you placed the arguments in that order.

1 Debate Topic: To be successful in life, one must study hard at school.

　Arguments: ⓐ The best jobs require applicants to have good grades at school.

　　　　　　ⓑ Studying hard allows people to develop important job skills and knowledge.

　　　　　　ⓒ More people graduate from college than ever before these days.

　　　　　　ⓓ People respect others who work and study hard.

Order: (　　) → (　　) → (　　) → (　　)

Explanation: _____

_____

2 Debate Topic: It is more important for children to study than to play with their friends.

　Arguments: ⓐ Playing with friends allows children to socialize and to meet new people.

　　　　　　ⓑ If children only study, they can become too bored.

　　　　　　ⓒ Children get lots of exercise when they play with others.

　　　　　　ⓓ Playing allows children to relieve their stress, and this helps them study better.

Order: (　　) → (　　) → (　　) → (　　)

Explanation: _____

_____

Unit 01 B Debating the Topic

Creating Your Debate

Motion: Afterschool academies help students and nations become more successful.

What are your arguments? Get into two groups and plan for the debate. Decide whether your team is FOR (agree) or AGAINST (disagree) the motion. Then, create your ARE: Argument, Reason, and Example. Use the example arguments below and the research from your workbook to help create your arguments.

■ Example Arguments

FOR

Argument

Afterschool academies help students gain valuable academic skills.

Reason

Students cannot learn enough information at school. Afterschool academies offer students extra instruction in key subjects such as math and English. This helps them be admitted to better high schools and colleges.

Example

Nearly all the students at Korea's best high schools and colleges attend many private academies. This extra studying helps these students get ahead of their peers.

AGAINST

Argument

Afterschool academies can cause financial problems for families.

Reason

A single academy usually costs from 100 to 1,000 dollars a month. To cover these costs, parents often have to work overtime or get extra jobs. This gives them less time to spend with their children.

Example

Many fathers work up to 12 hours a day, six days a week to earn enough money to pay for their children's academies.

■ Arguments FOR/AGAINST the Motion

ARGUMENT 1	ARGUMENT 2	ARGUMENT 3
Argument	**Argument**	**Argument**
Reason	**Reason**	**Reason**
Example	**Example**	**Example**

Actual Debate

Now, it's time to debate. Use the flow chart below to help you organize the debate.
The introductory expressions have been provided to help you. Put your arguments in logical order and make clear rebuttals to the opposing team's arguments.

Agree Opening Statement
It is our belief that _____ _____ is beneficial.

Disagree Opening Statement
The con team feels that _____ _____ should be banned.

Agree Argument 1
For our opening argument, _____
_____
_____
_____
_____.

Rebuttal 1
Our opponents believe that _____
_____.
Even so, _____.

Disagree Argument 1
The primary shortcoming of _____ is
_____.

Rebuttal 1
Your opinion that _____
_____ is mistaken.
_____.

Rebuttal 2
It is wrong to assume that _____
_____.

Agree Argument 2
For our second argument, _____
_____.

Disagree Argument 2
It is also necessary to consider that _____
_____
_____.

Rebuttal 2
Our team disagrees that _____
_____.

Rebuttal 3
The opposing team claims that _____
_____.

Agree Argument 3
Our final argument is _____
_____
_____.

Disagree Argument 3
The final point we would like to make against this topic is _____
_____.

Agree Closing Statement
While the opposing team gave fine arguments, we ultimately believe that _____
_____.

Disagree Closing Statement
In conclusion, we disagree that _____
_____
_____.

Sum Up the Debate

Finish the debate summary.

AGREEING SIDE'S ARGUMENT

Today's debate motion was _____.

The pro team argued _____.

Their first argument was _____.

They supported this by explaining that _____
_____.

Next, the team posited _____

Their claim was supported by _____
_____.

Finally, they reasoned _____.

For example, _____
_____.

DISAGREEING SIDE'S ARGUMENT

The second team argued differently. They felt _____
_____.

Their opening argument was _____.

Their supporting idea was _____
_____.

Their next argument was _____

For example, _____
_____.

Their final point was _____.

This was explained by _____
_____.

21

Unit 02 Genetically Modified Foods

WARM-UP

A. Discuss the following questions as a class.

1. What do you see in the picture above?
2. How can genetically modifying the foods we eat benefit us?
3. Do you think genetically modifying foods can have any negative side effects?

B. Answer the following questions with a partner.

1. Why do you think scientists genetically modify our foods?
2. Who would benefit the most from genetically modified foods?
3. Would you be comfortable eating foods that have been genetically modified? Explain.

Unit 02 A Learning about the Topic

Should scientists be allowed to modify the foods we eat?

Read the passage and underline the main ideas.   Track 04

Scientists first discovered that it is possible to transfer DNA between **organisms** in 1946. Nearly five decades later, this discovery led to the creation of the first genetically modified (GM) foods. Today, nearly all of the most common foods are genetically modified. These include tomatoes, corn, and cheese. GM foods offer several advantages over traditionally grown crops, yet the use of GM foods remains controversial. Is it okay for scientists to modify the foods we eat?

The idea to modify crops to create new varieties is not new. For centuries, farmers have crossbred crops in order to make new crops with better **characteristics**. Scientists can now modify foods at the genetic level, making it easy to create new types of crops. Some critics claim that modifying crops is unnatural. The fact is that nature creates new species all the time in a process called **mutation**. Genetically modifying crops is simply a way for scientists to help nature do its work more quickly. Best of all, GM foods are healthier and cheaper than naturally grown foods. The primary example is golden rice, which has lots of vitamin A. Other GM foods can be designed to grow larger and more quickly, which lowers the prices of the foods.

In spite of the benefits of GM foods, many people still worry about their use. One common argument is that there is not enough research about the long-term effects of GM foods. Many of the studies on the effects of GM foods have only been short-term ones. Scientists still do not know how GM foods can affect the body after many years of **consumption**. Critics also worry that the regulation of GM foods may be biased. They fear the companies testing GM foods may **overlook** their side effects in order to have them approved for use as food. We are also not sure how GM foods can affect the environment. It may be possible that GM foods can cause unexpected mutations to the soil and to other crops.

Vocabulary Check

Choose the correct word for each definition.

| organism | characteristic | mutation | consumption | overlook |

1 not to see or pay attention to _____
2 a change in the genes of a living thing _____
3 an individual living thing _____
4 showing something typical of a group or person _____
5 the act of eating or drinking something _____

Comprehension Questions

Check the correct answer for each question.

1 What major scientific event happened in 1946?
- ☐ The creation of the first genetically modified foods
- ☐ The first transfer of DNA between organisms

2 Why is it wrong to argue that modifying crops is unnatural?
- ☐ Because the mutation of organisms occurs in nature
- ☐ Because farmers have been crossbreeding crops for centuries

3 How are GM foods better than traditionally grown foods?
- ☐ They grow more quickly in more types of environments.
- ☐ They are more nutritious and can grow larger.

4 Why are scientists unsure of how GM foods can affect the body in the long term?
- ☐ Because only short-term studies of the effects of GM foods have been conducted
- ☐ Because testers may overlook the side effects of GM foods to have them approved

Questions for Debate

Think of and share ideas to explore the debatable issues in the article. Be sure to state your opinion clearly and to provide one supporting idea for each opinion.

1. How can GM foods benefit people who live in countries where there is not enough food to eat?

   It is my belief that _____
   _____.

   For instance, _____
   _____.

2. In your opinion, why did farmers modify crops in the first place?

   From my perspective, it seems that _____
   _____.

   I believe this because _____
   _____.

3. How can food companies profit from GM foods?

   I feel that _____
   _____.

   Let me illustrate this by mentioning _____
   _____.

4. Do you think genetically modifying foods can affect the body differently than natural foods?

   I think that _____
   _____.

   For example, _____
   _____.

5. Since more people want organically grown foods today, do you think GM foods can be popular?

   The fact of the matter is _____
   _____.

   To explain further, _____
   _____.

Opinion Examples

Look at the opinion examples about the motion below and answer the questions.

> **Motion: Genetically modifying foods should be allowed to continue.**

Opinion A Track 05

More than one billion people in our world today go without enough food. To help correct this problem, scientists must continue to genetically modify foods. With genetically modified foods, it is possible to create more food from the same amount of crops. For instance, genetically modified wheat produces almost three times more wheat than naturally grown wheat. There's also the added benefit of more nutritious crops. Scientists can add more vitamins and minerals to GM crops. The best example is golden rice. It has lots of vitamin A. It could save the lives of the millions of children who die from malnutrition every year.

Opinion B Track 06

GM foods sound like a good idea in theory. However, they belong in the laboratory, not in the supermarket. So far, studies of GM foods have found them to be safe in the short term. The problem is that no studies have been conducted on people for longer than six months. Scientists still have no idea how GM foods can affect us in the long term. Modifying crops could also cause mutations that no one expects or wants. To give an example, unwanted plants such as weeds can become immune to chemical weed killers. This would create a lot of problems for farmers.

1 Underline the main idea of each opinion.

2 Which opinion is for the topic? Which one is against it?
- FOR: _____
- AGAINST: _____

3 What supporting ideas does each opinion give?
- Opinion A: _____
- Opinion B: _____

4 Create one more supporting idea for each argument.
- Opinion A: _____
- Opinion B: _____

Skills for Debate

Read and learn how to organize your supporting arguments.

How Can You Organize Your Supporting Arguments?

Another possible way to organize your arguments is to have them **build upon each other**. Your first argument presents an idea that you explain in more depth in your second argument. Your third argument can present another idea related to the first two arguments. Organizing your arguments this way gives your ideas more **coherence**. Having your arguments build upon each other also shows the debate judges that you have **considered the topic carefully**.

Practicing Debate Skills

Read the debate topics below. The first supporting argument for each side has been given for you. Come up with two more supporting arguments that build upon the first supporting argument.

1 National governments should provide food for people who cannot afford to buy it themselves.

FOR
- Governments have a responsibility to care for their citizens.
- _____
- _____

AGAINST
- People are less motivated to work if the government gives too much free assistance.
- _____
- _____

2 Food makers should be required to put labels on GM foods.

FOR
- Consumers have a right to know what ingredients go into their foods.
- _____
- _____

AGAINST
- GM organisms that are used in foods are already tested as safe to eat.
- _____
- _____

Unit 02 B Debating the Topic

Creating Your Debate

Motion: Genetically modifying foods should be allowed to continue.

What are your arguments? Get into two groups and plan for the debate. Decide whether your team is FOR (agree) or AGAINST (disagree) the motion. Then, create your ARE: Argument, Reason, and Example. Use the example arguments below and the research from your workbook to help create your arguments.

■ **Example Arguments**

FOR

Argument

Genetically modifying foods is not any different from crossbreeding crops.

Reason

When scientists genetically modify food, they are mixing the characteristics of existing crops. The same thing happens when farmers crossbreed the crops they grow.

Example

Flower growers created pink roses by crossbreeding red roses and white roses. This is done simply by adding the pollen from one flower to the other flower. GM foods are created the same way but at a molecular level.

AGAINST

Argument

GM foods could be potentially dangerous to our health.

Reason

Our bodies have evolved to digest the foods we eat over thousands of years. GM foods change the food at the genetic level. This could have serious consequences on our bodies.

Example

Even though GM foods such as golden rice have obvious health benefits, many of them have not been approved to be used as food. This shows that national governments do not believe that GM foods are safe enough to eat.

Arguments FOR/AGAINST the Motion

ARGUMENT 1

Argument

_____
_____
_____
_____
_____

Reason

_____
_____
_____
_____
_____

Example

_____
_____
_____
_____
_____

ARGUMENT 2

Argument

_____
_____
_____
_____
_____

Reason

_____
_____
_____
_____
_____

Example

_____
_____
_____
_____
_____

ARGUMENT 3

Argument

_____
_____
_____
_____
_____

Reason

_____
_____
_____
_____
_____

Example

_____
_____
_____
_____
_____

Actual Debate

Now, it's time to debate. Use the flow chart below to help you organize the debate.
The introductory expressions have been provided to help you. Put your arguments in logical order and make clear rebuttals to the opposing team's arguments.

Agree Opening Statement
Our opinion is that _____
_____ should be allowed.

Disagree Opening Statement
We disagree with the idea that _____
_____.

Agree Argument 1
For our first argument, we believe _____
_____
_____
_____
_____
_____.

Rebuttal 1
You claimed that _____
_____
_____.
However, _____.

Disagree Argument 1
As for our first argument, _____
_____
_____.

Rebuttal 1
Your team claims that _____
_____, but we believe that
_____.

Rebuttal 2
You incorrectly argue that _____
_____
_____.

Agree Argument 2
Second, it is definitely true that _____
_____
_____.

Disagree Argument 2
Instead, consider that _____
_____
_____.

Rebuttal 2
Even though _____,
we must point out that _____
_____.

Rebuttal 3
The opposing team incorrectly believes that _____
_____
_____.

Agree Argument 3
Our final argument is _____
_____.

Disagree Argument 3
Finally, it should be mentioned that _____
_____.

Agree Closing Statement
We, the members of the pro team, feel that _____
_____
_____.

Disagree Closing Statement
In brief, we disagree that _____
_____
_____.

Sum Up the Debate

Finish the debate summary.

AGREEING SIDE'S ARGUMENT

Our debate topic was _____.

The agreeing team's opinion was _____.

For their opening argument, they said _____.

To support this, they explained that _____

_____.

Their second argument was _____.

To be specific, _____

_____.

The team concluded by arguing _____.

For instance, _____

_____.

DISAGREEING SIDE'S ARGUMENT

In contrast, the second team argued _____

_____.

They started by arguing that _____.

This argument was supported by _____

_____.

Second, they posited that _____.

They specifically mentioned _____

_____.

Their final argument was _____.

In detail, they explained that _____

_____.

Chapter 2

Developing Logical Supporting Reasons

Unit 03 Climate Change

Unit 04 Replacing Teachers with Computers

Unit 03: Climate Change

A. Discuss the following questions as a class.
1. What do you see in the picture above?
2. Which activities or events do you think cause climate change?
3. Do you think human activities have made climate change worse? Why or why not?

B. Answer the following questions with a partner.
1. What are some ways people can help stop climate change?
2. Do you think the Earth's climate can change because of natural causes?
3. In your opinion, is climate change a serious problem?

Unit 03 A Learning about the Topic

Should people worry about affecting the planet's climate?

Read the passage and underline the main ideas.

 Track 07

The Earth is getting hotter, and so is the debate surrounding climate change. Believers in climate change point to hundreds of scientific studies to support their ideas. At the same time, climate change skeptics point to the same evidence to argue that climate change is not occurring. What arguments do both sides make? Read on to find out.

Proponents of the climate change **theory** point to the fact that the Earth's carbon dioxide levels have increased dramatically since the 1800s. They claim this rise is the result of human activity. The rise in carbon dioxide has contributed to a rise in the overall temperature of the Earth. Climate models show that the average temperature of the Earth has risen about one degree Celsius in the past century. Many scientists believe this is due to human activity. The models also suggest that the temperature will rise another two degrees within the next 50 years. Despite this, some recent winters have had much more snowfall than usual. Higher carbon dioxide levels trap more **moisture** in the atmosphere. This can cause more snowfall to occur.

A significant number of people **deny** that any unusual climate change is occurring. One of their arguments is that the levels of carbon dioxide were much higher in the past. Several studies have found that carbon dioxide levels were up to 12 times higher millions of years ago. In spite of the high levels of carbon dioxide, life was still able to **thrive**. Another point is that the rise in temperature has not been **consistent**. Specifically, the average global temperature actually decreased between 1940 and 1975. This drop occurred even though carbon dioxide levels rose greatly during this time. There is also evidence that some plants benefit from increased levels of carbon dioxide. The current level of carbon dioxide in the atmosphere is around 400 parts per million. However, many greenhouses have carbon dioxide levels of more than 1,000 parts per million to help their plants grow.

Vocabulary Check

Choose the correct word for each definition.

| theory | moisture | deny | thrive | consistent |

1 to grow or live successfully _____
2 to say something is not true _____
3 a set of ideas to explain a fact or event _____
4 a small amount of liquid that makes something wet _____
5 continuing to happen in the same way _____

Comprehension Questions

Check the correct answer for each question.

1 What is the main cause of rising temperatures according to the climate change theory?
  ☐ The fact that the population levels have risen greatly in the past few decades
  ☐ The fact that carbon dioxide levels have increased because of human activities

2 How much do scientists think the temperature will rise in the next 50 years?
  ☐ about one degree Celsius
  ☐ two degrees Celsius

3 What is true about carbon dioxide levels in the Earth's atmosphere?
  ☐ They were 12 times higher millions of years ago.
  ☐ They are now higher than at any other time in history.

4 What happened between 1940 and 1975?
  ☐ The average global temperature decreased.
  ☐ Carbon dioxide levels stopped rising.

Questions for Debate

Think of and share ideas to explore the debatable issues in the article. Be sure to state your opinion clearly and to provide one supporting idea for each opinion.

1 What do you think the main factors that cause climate change are?

In my opinion, _____
_____.

The reason I say this is _____
_____.

2 What are some ways people can reduce carbon dioxide emissions?

I feel that _____
_____.

For instance, _____
_____.

3 Do you think the change in the Earth's climate could be due to natural causes?

From my perspective, it seems that _____
_____.

To go into detail, _____
_____.

4 How could serious changes in the Earth's temperature affect life on the planet?

It is my belief that _____
_____.

One example is _____
_____.

5 Do you believe supporters of climate change care only about the environment? Do they have other factors that motivate them?

My opinion is _____
_____.

The reason I believe this is _____
_____.

Opinion Examples

Look at the opinion examples about the motion below and answer the questions.

Motion: Climate change is a serious problem that needs to be addressed right away.

Opinion A Track 08

We need to work to stop climate change before it is too late. Since 1979, the size of the Arctic ice has shrunk by nearly 35 percent. This is due to global warming. Increased carbon dioxide levels have resulted in shorter winters and longer summers. Fortunately, there is a solution. Governments and businesses must do everything they can to reduce carbon dioxide emissions. They must develop alternative energy sources, like solar and hydrogen power. They must encourage people to take more public transportation and to eat less meat. By making small changes to our lives, we can reduce carbon dioxide levels and save the planet.

Opinion B Track 09

The idea that our lives could be ruined due to climate change is scary. Regardless, I am not convinced that global climate change is a serious problem. I read in my science book that nature produces 26 times as much carbon dioxide as humans do. This means that human activity contributes only a small amount to overall carbon dioxide levels. Scientists also argue that sea levels will continue to rise over the next 50 years. The fact is that no one can predict the future. Maybe sea levels will rise, or maybe they won't. We can't worry about something that may not even happen.

1 Underline the main idea of each opinion.

2 Which opinion is for the topic? Which one is against it?
- FOR: _____
- AGAINST: _____

3 What supporting ideas does each opinion give?
- Opinion A: _____
- Opinion B: _____

4 Create one more supporting idea for each argument.
- Opinion A: _____
- Opinion B: _____

Skills for Debate

Read and learn how to create logical supporting reasons.

How Can You Create Logical Supporting Reasons?

After creating and organizing your arguments, you must create your supporting logic. In general, you should have two to five sentences of supporting logic. Your logic should **clearly show** what your argument is about and why it is important. To do this, your logic must show **progression**. This is when **ideas build upon each other** to reach a conclusion about the argument. Therefore, the first step to creating good logic is to make sure every idea clearly follows the one before it.

Practicing Debate Skills

Read each of the arguments below and examine their logic. The first and last steps of the logic are provided. You must connect the first and last ideas with arguments that are clearly logical.
An example is given for you.

1 **Argument:** Daily homework assignments can decrease students' grades and performances.

   Logic: ⓐ Giving homework every day makes students very busy

   ⓑ <u>Students do not have enough time to play or relax.</u>

   ⓒ <u>This can make students very stressed.</u>

   ⓓ When students are stressed, they cannot focus well in school.

2 **Argument:** Keeping animals in zoos helps protect endangered species.

   Logic: ⓐ Species become endangered when their populations decrease very suddenly.

   ⓑ _____

   ⓒ _____

   ⓓ Therefore, zoos help animal populations stabilize and even increase.

3 **Argument:** Free public transportation could help reduce air pollution.

   Logic: ⓐ Automobiles are some of the biggest sources of pollution.

   ⓑ _____

   ⓒ _____

   ⓓ Making public transportation free will reduce the amount of pollution that is produced.

Unit 03 B Debating the Topic

Creating Your Debate

Motion: Climate change is a serious problem that needs to be addressed right away.

What are your arguments? Get into two groups and plan for the debate. Decide whether your team is FOR (agree) or AGAINST (disagree) the motion. Then, create your ARE: Argument, Reason, and Example. Use the example arguments below and the research from your workbook to help create your arguments.

■ Example Arguments

FOR	AGAINST
Argument	**Argument**
Rising sea levels could cause major changes to our cities.	A rise in carbon dioxide levels has not always caused a rise in temperatures.
Reason	**Reason**
Many of the world's major cities are located in low-lying areas. If sea levels rise another foot, most of these places could fall under water. Millions of people would lose their homes because of this.	Some climate models suggest that a rise in the Earth's carbon dioxide levels does not always result in higher temperatures. Sometimes temperatures have risen before carbon dioxide levels. In this case, carbon dioxide may not cause temperature increases.
Example	**Example**
Scientists at Columbia University's Earth Institute argue that sea levels could rise by more than seven meters by the year 2100. This would be enough to put London and Los Angeles under water.	Between 1940 and 1975, carbon dioxide levels increased. Nonetheless, average temperatures on the Earth stayed the same or even fell.

Arguments FOR/AGAINST the Motion

ARGUMENT 1

Argument

_____
_____
_____
_____
_____
_____

Reason

_____
_____
_____
_____
_____

Example

_____
_____
_____
_____
_____

ARGUMENT 2

Argument

_____
_____
_____
_____
_____
_____

Reason

_____
_____
_____
_____
_____

Example

_____
_____
_____
_____
_____

ARGUMENT 3

Argument

_____
_____
_____
_____
_____
_____

Reason

_____
_____
_____
_____
_____

Example

_____
_____
_____
_____
_____

Actual Debate

Now, it's time to debate. Use the flow chart below to help you organize the debate.
The introductory expressions have been provided to help you. Put your arguments in logical order and make clear rebuttals to the opposing team's arguments.

Agree Opening Statement
It is the opinion of the pro side that _____.

Agree Argument 1
To begin with, _____.

Rebuttal 1
Your opinion that _____ is mistaken.

Agree Argument 2
For our second argument, _____.

Rebuttal 2
You said that _____. But we think _____.

Agree Argument 3
For our last argument, let us point out that _____.

Agree Closing Statement
It is the pro team's opinion that _____.

Disagree Opening Statement
From our team's perspective, _____ _____ is not an issue to be concerned about.

Rebuttal 1
You claimed that _____.
However, _____.

Disagree Argument 1
As for our first argument, _____.

Rebuttal 2
You argue that _____, yet _____.

Disagree Argument 2
The next idea we would like you to think about is _____.

Rebuttal 3
In spite of your argument that _____, we believe _____.

Disagree Argument 3
The final point we would like to make against this topic is _____.

Disagree Closing Statement
Our overall opinion is that _____.

42

Sum Up the Debate

Finish the debate summary.

AGREEING SIDE'S ARGUMENT

The motion for this debate was _____.

The pro team argued _____.

For their opening argument, they stated _____.

They supported this by explaining that _____
_____.

Next, they explained _____.

In more detail, _____
_____.

Their final reason was _____.

For instance, _____
_____.

DISAGREEING SIDE'S ARGUMENT

The con side presented the opposite opinion. They stated _____
_____.

To start with, they claimed that _____.

They mentioned _____
_____ to support their claim.

For their second argument, they presented _____.

To be specific, _____
_____.

For their final argument, the con team mentioned _____.

For their example, they said _____
_____.

43

Unit 04: Replacing Teachers with Computers

A. Discuss the following questions as a class.
1. What do you see in the picture above?
2. How do computers help students learn in school?
3. How can computers make it more difficult for students to study?

B. Answer the following questions with a partner.
1. Do you believe teachers should allow students to use computers during class?
2. How can using computers affect the learning content students use?
3. What are some ways teachers educate students beyond academic learning?

Unit 04 A Learning about the Topic

Should computers replace teachers in classrooms?

Read the passage and underline the main ideas.   Track 10

Schools around the world are facing more and more budget cuts. In the past, school districts tried to cut expenses by reducing the number of teachers in each school. Now, some education experts are suggesting taking the next step: getting rid of teachers altogether. In their place, schools could use computers to educate students. Using computers instead of teachers may create a better learning environment, or it could ruin education as we know it.

There are several advantages to having computers replace teachers. For one, schools can be sure that all students learn from the same **curricula**. Currently, schools cannot be sure every teacher uses and covers the same material. If computers take the place of teachers, this will not be a problem. Another related benefit is that class time will be more **structured**. Classes conducted on the computer would follow specific teaching schedules. No class time would be wasted by having teachers chat with students about unrelated topics. In addition, using computers in classes will be cheaper than hiring teachers. Schools can purchase computers cheaply. They could hire aids at low wages to watch the classes. This will save underfunded schools lots of money in the long run.

While these advantages are undeniable, many are strongly against having computers replace teachers. One reason is that teacher-student **interaction** would be lost. Teachers develop personal and even emotional connections with their students. This human connection makes students feel more involved in their learning. Likewise, teachers provide lessons that are more than just academic. Effective teachers **instill** into students important life lessons. These include lessons about honesty, hard work, and respect. It is also important to consider that teachers provide students with different viewpoints. Online lessons created by a school board would only offer one perspective about a topic. In contrast, teachers can encourage discussion about topics presented in class materials. They offer views that question or **contradict** the school's learning material. These discussions broaden students' thinking.

Vocabulary Check

Choose the correct word for each definition.

| curriculum | structured | interaction | instill | contradict |

1 to say the opposite of what someone else said   _____
2 to cause someone to develop an attitude or opinion   _____
3 the act of talking and doing things with other people   _____
4 the courses taught by a school or college   _____
5 organized; planned   _____

Comprehension Questions

Check the correct answer for each question.

1 What have schools already tried to do in order to save money?
   ☐ Use more computers in the classroom
   ☐ Reduce the number of teachers at each school

2 Why would computers make class time more structured?
   ☐ Because classes would follow specific teaching schedules
   ☐ Because every class would use different learning material

3 What kinds of life lessons do students learn from their teachers? Choose TWO correct answers.
   ☐ hard work   ☐ respect
   ☐ saving money   ☐ politeness

4 In what way can teachers broaden students' thinking?
   ☐ They can explain the class materials in more detail than computers.
   ☐ They can offer different perspectives about the school's learning material.

Questions for Debate

Think of and share ideas to explore the debatable issues in the article. Be sure to state your opinion clearly and to provide one supporting idea for each opinion.

1. Do you think having lessons on the computer would make students more interested in their studies?

    It is my feeling that _____

    _____.

    To give an example, _____

    _____.

2. What advantages do computers have over books in terms of learning material?

    It is my opinion that _____

    _____.

    The reason is _____

    _____.

3. Is it a teacher's job to educate his or her students about life issues such as honesty? Explain.

    From my perspective, it seems that _____

    _____.

    I believe this because _____

    _____.

4. How could teachers still contribute to education even if computers replaced them in classrooms?

    It is my opinion that _____

    _____.

    Consider that _____

    _____.

5. Does the government provide enough funding to schools? Why or why not?

    My feeling is _____

    _____.

    For instance, _____

    _____.

47

Opinion Examples

Look at the opinion examples about the motion below and answer the questions.

Motion: Computers should take the place of teachers in classrooms.

Opinion A Track 11

It is finally time for technology to replace teachers in classrooms. There are many teachers who teach well, but it is too expensive to pay the salaries of these qualified teachers. Besides, if computers replace teachers, then the overall quality of instruction will improve. School districts could make sure that every class covers the same learning material at the same rate. Students can also benefit from more up-to-date learning material. Textbooks are expensive, and schools cannot afford to purchase updated ones regularly. When classes are conducted on computers, the material could be updated in the blink of an eye.

Opinion B Track 12

I'm shocked that people are even considering having computers replace teachers. To me, it is clear that teachers are essential for education. Teachers can motivate and inspire their students in ways that computers alone never can. They have passion, personality, and sincerity, which are all necessary to connect with students. Students can also learn multiple perspectives from their teachers. Computers would only present one curriculum for students. They would not have the chance to hear different opinions about topics. My fifth grade teacher Mrs. Holmes encouraged me to think critically in a way no computer ever could. For the sake of students everywhere, teachers must stay where they belong: in the classroom.

1 Underline the main idea of each opinion.

2 Which opinion is for the topic? Which one is against it?
- FOR: _____
- AGAINST: _____

3 What supporting ideas does each opinion give?
- Opinion A: _____
- Opinion B: _____

4 Create one more supporting idea for each argument.
- Opinion A: _____
- Opinion B: _____

Skills for Debate

Read and learn how to create logical supporting reasons.

How Can You Create Logical Supporting Reasons?

Not every supporting reason given during a debate is logical. Sometimes, debaters create arguments that are incorrect or do not make sense. These are called **logical fallacies**. To be a good debater, you must avoid using logical fallacies. At the same time, you must be able to point out errors in logic the other team makes. Here are some of the most common logical fallacies:

1. **argument to tradition:** arguing that something is right because it has been done for a long time
2. **argument by repetition:** repeating the same argument over and over
3. **sweeping generalization:** making a very broad statement and saying it is always true

Practicing Debate Skills

Read the flowing logical supporting reasons. Decide which type of logical fallacy each reason is. Finally, rewrite the fallacy so that it is logically correct.

1. Traditionally, women have not had jobs. They have always stayed at home. There is no reason that women today should work.
   - Fallacy Type: _____
   - Rewrite: _____

2. Women are physically weaker than men. Thus, no women should be allowed to serve in the military.
   - Fallacy Type: _____
   - Rewrite: _____

3. Working helps teenagers develop job skills. Having a job helps students improve their work skills. Therefore, teenagers must work.
   - Fallacy Type: _____
   - Rewrite: _____

Unit 04 B Debating the Topic

Creating Your Debate

Motion: Computers should take the place of teachers in classrooms.

What are your arguments? Get into two groups and plan for the debate. Decide whether your team is FOR (agree) or AGAINST (disagree) the motion. Then, create your ARE: Argument, Reason, and Example. Use the example arguments below and the research from your workbook to help create your arguments.

■ Example Arguments

FOR

Argument

Replacing teachers would allow schools to have more structured curricula.

Reason

Every teacher organizes his or her class differently. This means that students in every class learn different material. If classes are conducted through computers, a school district head office could design the same curricula for all classes. This makes learning more equal.

Example

One study found that the least effective teachers cover only 50 percent of the required learning material each year. Using computers could ensure that all students learn an equal amount of material.

AGAINST

Argument

Teachers inspire us to be better people in addition to offering academic lessons.

Reason

Along with parents, teachers are the most important adult role models in a child's life. Teachers often understand how children develop better than almost any other people. As such, teachers often provide students with important life lessons, such as honesty and hard work.

Example

The John F. Kennedy Center in Washington, D.C., presents the Stephen Sondheim Award for the most inspirational teacher of the year.

Arguments FOR/AGAINST the Motion

ARGUMENT 1

Argument

Reason

Example

ARGUMENT 2

Argument

Reason

Example

ARGUMENT 3

Argument

Reason

Example

Actual Debate

Now, it's time to debate. Use the flow chart below to help you organize the debate.
The introductory expressions have been provided to help you. Put your arguments in logical order and make clear rebuttals to the opposing team's arguments.

Agree Opening Statement
It is our belief that _____ is beneficial.

Agree Argument 1
For our first argument, we believe _____
_____
_____
_____
_____.

Rebuttal 1
The opposition argued that _____
_____,
but _____.

Agree Argument 2
Our second reason in favor of the argument is _____
_____.

Rebuttal 2
Even though _____
_____, we must point out that
_____.

Agree Argument 3
Our final argument is _____
_____.

Agree Closing Statement
We, the members of the pro team, feel that _____
_____.

Disagree Opening Statement
We disagree with the motion that _____
_____.

Rebuttal 1
Our opponents believe that _____
_____.
Even so, _____.

Disagree Argument 1
The primary shortcoming of _____
_____ is
_____.

Rebuttal 2
It is wrong to assume that _____
_____.

Disagree Argument 2
It is also necessary to consider that _____
_____
_____.

Rebuttal 3
The opposing team claims that _____
_____.

Disagree Argument 3
The final point we would like to make against this topic is _____
_____.

Disagree Closing Statement
In brief, we disagree that _____
_____.

Sum Up the Debate

Finish the debate summary.

AGREEING SIDE'S ARGUMENT

The topic of today's debate was _____.

The main opinion of the agreeing team was _____.

For their opening argument, they said _____.

To support this, they explained that _____

_____.

For their second argument, they presented _____

For instance, _____

_____.

Finally, they reasoned _____

To share their example, _____

_____.

DISAGREEING SIDE'S ARGUMENT

The con team presented a different opinion. They argued _____

_____.

Their opening argument was _____.

This argument was supported by _____

_____.

Second, they posited that _____.

They specifically mentioned _____

_____.

Their final argument was _____.

In detail, they explained that _____

_____.

Chapter 3

Developing Effective Supporting Reasons

Unit 05 Using CCTVs in Public Places

Unit 06 Celebrity Salaries

Unit 05: Using CCTVs in Public Places

WARM-UP

A. Discuss the following questions as a class.
1. What do you see in the picture above?
2. Have you seen similar-looking cameras before? If so, where did you see them?
3. Why do you think a camera was installed in this place?

B. Answer the following questions with a partner.
1. Do you think cities should be allowed to install cameras everywhere? Why or why not?
2. How do you think criminals feel whenever they see security cameras?
3. How do you think security cameras can be used in harmful ways?

Unit 05 A Learning about the Topic

Should governments be allowed to use CCTVs in public places?

Read the passage and underline the main ideas.  Track 13

The United Kingdom has over 4.2 million closed-circuit television (CCTV) cameras. That is more than any other country. The idea behind CCTV systems is that they help **deter** crime. Yet a large number of people feel that CCTVs simply offer a way for governments to spy on their people. Are CCTVs an invasion of privacy, or can they actually make society safer?

The problems with CCTVs are undeniable. CCTVs take away our freedom of privacy. Most CCTV cameras are installed in busy downtown areas and on public transportation. Using these cameras, the government is able to track the movement of **innocent** citizens without their knowledge or **consent**. This could be acceptable if CCTVs definitely reduced crime. Unfortunately, most evidence suggests that they have almost no impact on crime rates. One study found that CCTV footage helped solve only 1 percent of violent crimes. Part of this may be due to the fact that footage from CCTVs is rarely usable. The picture quality is often poor. This makes it difficult to recognize faces or to track criminals by using CCTV footage. Another study discovered that violent crimes actually increased after CCTVs were installed. When cities install security cameras, they have fewer police officers patrolling the streets.

There are still ways CCTVs have been used to make society safer. Whenever potential criminals see CCTV cameras, they are less likely to commit crime. They decide there is too much risk of getting caught because of the cameras. The reason for this is that police and security forces can monitor CCTV footage in real time. They can act quickly when they see **suspicious** activity and stop crimes from happening. Even after a major crime has occurred, CCTVs still play a **valuable** role. Following the Boston Marathon Bombings in 2013, law enforcement officials reviewed CCTV footage from downtown Boston. They used it to see the faces of the criminals responsible for the bombings. Thanks to CCTVs, the bombers were captured in just a few days.

Vocabulary Check

Choose the correct word for each definition.

| deter | innocent | consent | suspicious | valuable |

1 to prevent something from happening _____
2 agreement to do or allow something _____
3 causing a feeling that someone is behaving wrongly _____
4 not guilty of a crime or other wrong act _____
5 very useful or helpful _____

Comprehension Questions

Check the correct answer for each question.

1 What is the original reason for installing CCTV systems?
   - ☐ To allow governments to spy on their people
   - ☐ To help deter criminal activities

2 Why has CCTV footage helped to solve such a small number of crimes?
   - ☐ Because the video quality is often too poor for police to track criminals
   - ☐ Because most cities do not have enough CCTV cameras installed in high-crime areas

3 How does monitoring CCTV footage in real time help police and security forces?
   - ☐ They can see suspicious activity and act quickly to stop crimes.
   - ☐ They can warn potential criminals not to break the law.

4 In what way did law enforcement use CCTV systems after the Boston Marathon Bombings?
   - ☐ They used the footage from CCTVs to see what the bombers looked like.
   - ☐ They reviewed CCTV footage from downtown Boston to see where the bombers lived.

Questions for Debate

Think of and share ideas to explore the debatable issues in the article. Be sure to state your opinion clearly and to provide one supporting idea for each opinion.

1 Do you feel safer whenever you see a CCTV camera? Why or why not?

I feel that _____.

To explain in more detail, _____.

2 In what ways are ordinary citizens affected by CCTV cameras?

It is my belief that _____.

For instance, _____.

3 What do you think the main limitations of CCTV camera systems are?

I believe that _____.

The reason I feel this way is _____.

4 Other than installing CCTVs, how can officials help prevent crimes from happening?

To me it seems that _____.

To give an example, _____.

5 In your opinion, do you think there will be more or fewer CCTV systems in the future?

My opinion is _____.

Specifically, _____.

Opinion Examples

Look at the opinion examples about the motion below and answer the questions.

Motion: CCTV systems are an invasion of privacy and should be outlawed.

Opinion A Track 14

Not many people like CCTVs, but they are necessary in today's society. Every second, there are hundreds of crimes being committed. The police cannot be everywhere all the time to stop all crimes. Even though CCTVs cannot cover every single area in a city, they give police extra sets of eyes so that they can monitor more places at once. One common criticism of CCTVs is that they are used to record ordinary citizens. However, if you are not doing anything wrong, then you don't have any reason to fear being recorded. CCTVs are simply the best way we have to keep everybody safe.

Opinion B Track 15

It is wrong to assume that CCTVs help deter crime. The best way to stop crime is not installing more CCTVs. It is hiring more police officers to patrol the streets. Police officers have a powerful presence. Criminals are genuinely afraid to break the law if they see police officers. One study found that increasing the number of police officers in a city by half reduces violent crime rates by 15 percent. This study also found that citizens feel safer when more police are on the street. The same cannot be said of CCTV cameras. Most research suggests that people worry they are being secretly monitored by CCTVs.

1 Underline the main idea of each opinion.

2 Which opinion is for the topic? Which one is against it?

- FOR: _____
- AGAINST: _____

3 What supporting ideas does each opinion give?

- Opinion A: _____
- Opinion B: _____

4 Create one more supporting idea for each argument.

- Opinion A: _____
- Opinion B: _____

Skills for Debate

Read and learn how to create effective supporting reasons.

How Can You Create Effective Supporting Reasons?

Effective supporting reasons must have three characteristics. First, they must explain **what** your argument is about. Provide a little bit of detail about each argument to make the meaning clear. Next, your reasons should explain **why** your argument is relevant. It is necessary for your reasons to make it clear that your argument is closely related to the motion. Finally, your reasons must illustrate **how** your argument matters. Talk about what happens to the world or society because of your argument. If you answer these three questions, your reasons will be logical.

Practicing Debate Skills

Read the arguments below. Create supporting reasons for each argument. Make sure that your ideas show progression.

1. Climate change occurs naturally and is healthy for the Earth.
    - what: Climate records show that the Earth goes through major climate changes every few thousand years.
    - why: This is important to point out because it suggests that the current climate change is not unusual.
    - how: Therefore, we do not need to be concerned about the current warming of the planet.

2. Older people are more effective leaders because they have more life experience.
    - what: _____
    - why: _____
    - how: _____

3. Saving money allows us to live more comfortable lives in the future.
    - what: _____
    - why: _____
    - how: _____

Unit 05 B Debating the Topic

Creating Your Debate

Motion: CCTV systems are an invasion of privacy and should be outlawed.

What are your arguments? Get into two groups and plan for the debate. Decide whether your team is FOR (agree) or AGAINST (disagree) the motion. Then, create your ARE: Argument, Reason, and Example. Use the example arguments below and the research from your workbook to help create your arguments.

- **Example Arguments**

FOR

Argument

CCTVs take away people's right to privacy.

Reason

Innocent citizens should be allowed to maintain their privacy in public places. The government has no right to monitor members of the public at all times.

Example

Article 12 of the Universal Declaration of Human Rights states that people should not have their right to privacy taken away. CCTV systems violate this right.

AGAINST

Argument

CCTV cameras help police catch criminals.

Reason

CCTV cameras can record evidence when there are no eyewitnesses. This video evidence is very useful for catching criminals.

Example

Last year, my bicycle was stolen from in front of my apartment building. Police were able to use the CCTV footage from the apartment's cameras to track down the thief, so I got my bike back.

■ Arguments FOR/AGAINST the Motion

ARGUMENT 1

Argument
_____
_____
_____
_____
_____
_____

Reason
_____
_____
_____
_____
_____

Example
_____
_____
_____
_____
_____
_____

ARGUMENT 2

Argument
_____
_____
_____
_____
_____
_____

Reason
_____
_____
_____
_____
_____

Example
_____
_____
_____
_____
_____
_____

ARGUMENT 3

Argument
_____
_____
_____
_____
_____
_____

Reason
_____
_____
_____
_____
_____

Example
_____
_____
_____
_____
_____
_____

Actual Debate

Now, it's time to debate. Use the flow chart below to help you organize the debate.
The introductory expressions have been provided to help you. Put your arguments in logical order and make clear rebuttals to the opposing team's arguments.

Agree Opening Statement
We, the members of the pro team, believe that _____ _____ _____ is beneficial.

Agree Argument 1
To begin with, _____ _____ _____ _____ _____.

Rebuttal 1
Your team claims that _____ _____, yet _____ _____.

Agree Argument 2
We also support this motion because ____ _____ _____.

Rebuttal 2
Our team disagrees that _____ _____ _____.

Agree Argument 3
Our final argument is _____ _____ _____ _____.

Agree Closing Statement
To conclude, the proposition believes that _____ _____.

Disagree Opening Statement
The disadvantages of _____ _____ _____ outweigh the benefits.

Rebuttal 1
It is the opposing team's belief that _____ _____ _____.
However, _____.

Disagree Argument 1
The primary shortcoming of _____ is _____ _____.

Rebuttal 2
It is wrong to assume that _____ _____ because _____ _____.

Disagree Argument 2
The next idea we would like you to consider is _____ _____.

Rebuttal 3
The opposing team claims that _____ _____ _____.

Disagree Argument 3
The final point we would like to make against this topic is _____ _____ _____.

Disagree Closing Statement
In summation, _____ _____ _____.

Sum Up the Debate

Finish the debate summary.

AGREEING SIDE'S ARGUMENT

Our debate topic was _____.

The opinion of the first team was _____.

For their opening argument, they said _____.

To support this, they explained that _____

_____.

Second, they claimed _____.

For example, _____

_____.

Their closing argument was _____.

They mentioned _____

_____ to support their argument.

DISAGREEING SIDE'S ARGUMENT

In contrast, the con team claimed _____

_____.

For their opening argument _____.

This argument was supported by _____

_____.

Second, they posited that _____.

They specifically mentioned _____

_____.

Their final argument was _____.

In detail, they explained that _____

_____.

Unit 06 Celebrity Salaries

A. Discuss the following questions as a class.
1. What do you see in the picture above?
2. Why do you think people are taking pictures of the woman?
3. How does the woman probably feel about being asked for her autograph?

B. Answer the following questions with a partner.
1. Who are some of your favorite actors, singers, or athletes?
2. In your opinion, are entertainers important to society?
3. Do you think people should earn more money if they are famous?

Unit 06 A Learning about the Topic

Should entertainers and athletes earn such high salaries?

Read the passage and underline the main ideas. Track 16

In 2012, movie star Tom Cruise earned 75 million dollars. This is 15,000 times more than what the average worker in the United States earns every year. Entertainers such as Tom Cruise help companies make huge **profits**, but it still may not be appropriate to pay entertainers such huge amounts of money.

For many reasons, entertainers are paid far too much for the work they do. First of all, entertainers are not necessary. Everybody enjoys watching his or her favorite actors or athletes perform, but people could still live without them. In contrast, jobs such as teacher, doctor, and trash collector are far more important to society. People who do these essential jobs should make a lot of money, not entertainers. Entertainers also promote unrealistic images of money and wealth. **Tabloids** often feature news stories about celebrities buying homes that cost millions of dollars. This is far beyond what most people will ever be able to afford. Nevertheless, many normal people try to copy the lifestyles of popular entertainers. For instance, they buy overpriced clothing and cars. This causes them to waste their money and to go into **debt**.

Despite these arguments, many people believe that paying high salaries to entertainers is **justified**. Entertainers have obvious special talents. Whenever people see a basketball player slam dunk or an actor perform an emotional scene, they think that these entertainers are very gifted. For this reason, most people think entertainers should be paid highly. Furthermore, entertainers make millions of people happy with their talents. Since entertainers affect the lives of so many people, they should earn high salaries. We must also remember that entertainers help generate money for other people. When Michael Jordan began playing for the Chicago Bulls, ticket sales increased. Ticket sales eventually **quadrupled** because of Michael Jordan's performance. Entertainers such as Michael Jordan help businesses make millions of dollars in income. In this way, their high salaries are their fair share of the money their work generates.

Vocabulary Check

Choose the correct word for each definition.

| profit | tabloid | debt | justified | quadruple |

1. to become four times bigger in number or amount _____
2. the state of owing money to someone or something _____
3. money that a business makes after expenses _____
4. a newspaper that covers stories about celebrities _____
5. having a good reason for doing something _____

Comprehension Questions

Check the correct answer for each question.

1. How much money did Tom Cruise earn in 2012?
   - ☐ 15,000 dollars
   - ☐ 75 million dollars

2. What does the passage say about teachers and doctors?
   - ☐ They do the most important work in society.
   - ☐ They should be paid more than entertainers.

3. How do entertainers cause people to go into debt?
   - ☐ They require people to spend too much money on movie tickets.
   - ☐ People buy overpriced products to copy their lifestyles.

4. What happened when Michael Jordan played for the Chicago Bulls?
   - ☐ He helped ticket sales increase four times.
   - ☐ He became the most popular player on the team.

Questions for Debate

Think of and share ideas to explore the debatable issues in the article. Be sure to state your opinion clearly and to provide one supporting idea for each opinion.

1. What are the differences between working as an entertainer and doing other jobs?

   My belief is _____
   _____.

   The reason I feel this way is _____
   _____.

2. Do you think entertainers always made huge amounts of money? Explain.

   I think that _____
   _____.

   For example, _____
   _____.

3. Does the work entertainers do benefit society? Why or why not?

   As far as I'm concerned, _____
   _____.

   For instance, _____
   _____.

4. What are some other jobs that pay very high salaries? What do most people think about these jobs?

   Some of these include _____
   _____.

   To go into more detail, _____
   _____.

5. Should all people in a society be paid about the same amount of money for the work they do? Why?

   My thoughts are _____
   _____.

   I believe this since _____
   _____.

Opinion Examples

Look at the opinion examples about the motion below and answer the questions.

Motion: Entertainers and athletes earn too much money and should be paid less.

Opinion A Track 17

To me, it seems that entertainers earn far too much money. Professional actors and athletes work hard, but so do workers with other jobs. In fact, many regular workers put in more hours than most entertainers. A famous actor may only film one big movie each year. This usually takes two or three months of work. Compare this to office workers, who are at their jobs 12 months a year. Moreover, entertainers are not necessary. Society can still function without movie stars, singers, and athletes. The work they do isn't that important, so they should not be paid that much money.

Opinion B Track 18

Actors and athletes make very high salaries, but their high paychecks are justified. After all, these entertainers affect the lives of millions of people. It is silly to compare an office worker that nobody knows to a world famous entertainer. Entertainers do work that has a large influence on society. Yes, other jobs such as doctor and farmer may be important in our daily lives. All the same, entertainers still shape culture. For this reason, entertainers generate lots of money for their companies. Since celebrities help generate millions of dollars for companies, they have every right to demand high salaries for themselves.

1 Underline the main idea of each opinion.

2 Which opinion is for the topic? Which one is against it?
- FOR: _____
- AGAINST: _____

3 What supporting ideas does each opinion give?
- Opinion A: _____
- Opinion B: _____

4 Create one more supporting idea for each argument.
- Opinion A: _____
- Opinion B: _____

Skills for Debate

Read and learn how to create effective supporting reasons.

How Can You Create Effective Supporting Reasons?

In addition to explaining what, why, and how, your supporting reasons can present your ideas in different ways. One effective method is to explain directly **why your argument is correct**. You can do this by listing short **ideas** and **examples**. Or you can present a **logical argument** for your side. Alternatively, you can **list problems with the opposing argument**. You can explain why the opposite idea is not effective or creates problems. At the end of your logic, you can describe how your argument is better. Try using all these types of supporting reasons to give your debate **variety**.

Practicing Debate Skills

Read the debate arguments below. For each argument, create logic that lists examples and ideas in favor of the argument. Then, list problems with the opposite argument. Some ideas have been given to help you.

1 **Debate Topic:** People pay too much attention to the private lives of celebrities.
   Argument: It is more important for people to focus on their own problems.

List of Ideas in Favor of the Argument	Problems with the Opposite Argument
• Most people have a lot of issues they must deal with each day.	• The lives of celebrities have little to do with the lives of regular people.
• _____	• _____
• _____	• _____

2 **Debate Topic:** Celebrities are a bad influence on children.
   Argument: Many celebrities behave in ways that are inappropriate.

List of Ideas in Favor of the Argument	Problems with the Opposite Argument
• Children need to have strong, positive role models in their lives.	• Celebrities often wear shocking clothing and make controversial comments.
• _____	• _____
• _____	• _____

Unit 06 B Debating the Topic

Creating Your Debate

> **Motion: Entertainers and athletes earn too much money and should be paid less.**

What are your arguments? Get into two groups and plan for the debate. Decide whether your team is FOR (agree) or AGAINST (disagree) the motion. Then, create your ARE: Argument, Reason, and Example. Use the example arguments below and the research from your workbook to help create your arguments.

■ Example Arguments

FOR

Argument

Entertainers are paid huge amounts of money for unimportant work.

Reason

Entertainers can make millions of dollars in a single year. This is more money than most people earn in their entire lives. Their high salaries would be justifiable if their work were critically important. However, it is not.

Example

Before the 20th century, being an entertainer was not considered a respectable job. Most entertainers made little money. Even professional athletes were poorly paid until the 1970s.

AGAINST

Argument

Professional entertainers and athletes help the companies they work for make lots of money, so they should be paid well.

Reason

Individual actors and entertainers can greatly influence the success of a movie or sporting event. For this reason, they should earn a lot of money.

Example

Actors and athletes are paid based on tickets sales. Film star Keanu Reeves earned $156 million for *The Matrix* films by taking a percentage of the ticket sales. The films recorded over $1 billion in total sales.

Arguments FOR/AGAINST the Motion

ARGUMENT 1	ARGUMENT 2	ARGUMENT 3
Argument	**Argument**	**Argument**
Reason	**Reason**	**Reason**
Example	**Example**	**Example**

Actual Debate

Now, it's time to debate. Use the flow chart below to help you organize the debate.
The introductory expressions have been provided to help you. Put your arguments in logical order and make clear rebuttals to the opposing team's arguments.

Agree Opening Statement
We, the members of the pro team, believe that _____
_____
_____.

Disagree Opening Statement
Unlike the pro team, we feel that _____
_____
_____.

Agree Argument 1
Our first argument is that _____
_____
_____
_____
_____.

Rebuttal 1
Your team claims that _____
_____. However,
_____
_____.

Disagree Argument 1
To give our first argument, _____
_____
_____.

Rebuttal 1
Your team claims that _____
_____,
yet _____
_____.

Agree Argument 2
We also support this motion because _____
_____
_____.

Rebuttal 2
Your team wrongly claims that _____
_____
_____.

Disagree Argument 2
In addition, we believe that _____
_____
_____.

Rebuttal 2
You stated that _____
_____. Nevertheless, _____
_____
_____.

Agree Argument 3
For our final argument, let us point out that _____
_____
_____.

Rebuttal 3
In spite of your argument that _____
_____, we believe
_____
_____.

Disagree Argument 3
To give our last argument, _____
_____
_____.

Agree Closing Statement
On the whole, our team contends that _____
_____
_____.

Disagree Closing Statement
To sum up, it is the con team's belief that _____
_____
_____.

Sum Up the Debate

Finish the debate summary.

AGREEING SIDE'S ARGUMENT

Today's motion was about the topic _____.

The agreeing team's opinion was _____.

For their opening argument, they said _____.

To support this, they explained that _____
_____.

Next, they argued _____.

In more detail, _____
_____.

Their final reason was _____.

Specifically, _____
_____.

DISAGREEING SIDE'S ARGUMENT

The con team presented a different opinion _____
_____.

Their opening argument was _____.

This argument was supported by _____
_____.

Second, they posited that _____.

They specifically mentioned _____
_____.

Their final argument was _____.

In detail, they explained that _____
_____.

Chapter 4

Giving Supporting Examples

Unit 07 Punishment for Criminals

Unit 08 Cosmetic Plastic Surgery

Unit 07 Punishment for Criminals

A. Discuss the following questions as a class.
1. What do you see in the picture above?
2. How do you think the man feels about his situation? Why?
3. Do you think criminals should be kept in harsh conditions like the prisoner above?

B. Answer the following questions with a partner.
1. What are some of the reasons people break the law in the first place?
2. Do you think sending criminals to live with other criminals in prison is an effective way to punish them? Explain.
3. Besides prison, what are some other ways to punish criminals?

Unit 07   A   Learning about the Topic

Should criminals be sent to prison as punishment?

Read the passage and underline the main ideas.

 Track 19

Within three years of leaving prison, more than half of prisoners commit more crimes and are sent back to prison. If prison were an effective form of punishment, why would so many prisoners continue to break the law? This is the question that many lawmakers are asking today. Instead of prison, they suggest alternative methods to **discourage** criminal behavior. It is possible these methods can be more effective at punishing criminals.

Most sociologists agree that people's behavior is largely shaped by their surroundings. Prisons are very violent and dangerous places. Therefore, the criminals sent to prison become more violent and dangerous themselves. This relates to a second problem of prisons: They do little to correct the problems that lead criminals to break the law in the first place. Many criminals break the law because they cannot get good-paying jobs. This is due to the fact that most lawbreakers lack formal education. Prisoners who receive more education while in prison are far less likely to break laws in the future. Yet very few prisons allow their prisoners to receive an education. Even though prisons do little to **rehabilitate** prisoners, they are very expensive to operate. United States prisons spend over $30,000 per **inmate** each year.

For many law enforcement authorities, prison is the most effective way to punish criminals. For one, prison removes dangerous criminals from society. Reducing the number of criminals in society leads to a reduction in the overall crime rate. In this way, prison makes society safer by getting lawbreakers off the streets. Another argument in favor of prison is that it is a deterrent against crime. Prison is a **terrifying** place, so potential criminals will be afraid to break the law. In addition, for serious criminals, being sent to prison may be the only appropriate punishment. These hardened criminals are unlikely to respond to counseling and other types of **therapy**. They are likely to continue breaking the law even after receiving rehabilitation. The only appropriate punishment is the harsh environment of prison.

Vocabulary Check

Choose the correct word for each definition.

| discourage | rehabilitate | inmate | terrifying | therapy |

1 to teach prisoners how to lead normal, productive lives _____
2 to make people not want to do something _____
3 a person serving time in jail; a prisoner _____
4 the treatment of problems of the body and mind _____
5 causing great fear _____

Comprehension Questions

Check the correct answer for each question.

1 What is true about prisoners after they leave prison?
   ☐ Most of them get proper jobs and become productive members of society.
   ☐ More than half of them commit more crimes and return to prison.

2 Why do most criminals break the law?
   ☐ Because they want to hurt other people
   ☐ Because they cannot get good-paying jobs

3 How can prisons make sure that prisoners do not break laws in the future?
   ☐ By spending more money on each inmate
   ☐ By giving them a formal education

4 How do prisons help reduce the overall crime rate?
   ☐ They reduce the number of criminals in society.
   ☐ They make criminals afraid to break the law.

Questions for Debate

Think of and share ideas to explore the debatable issues in the article. Be sure to state your opinion clearly and to provide one supporting idea for each opinion.

1. Do you think having longer jail sentences will reduce the number of criminals in society? Explain.

   I think that _____
   _____.

   For example, _____
   _____.

2. In your experience, are you less likely to misbehave if you will get a harsh punishment? Explain.

   My experience is _____
   _____.

   This is due to the fact that _____
   _____.

3. What kind of background and family do most criminals come from? Why is this important?

   As far as I know, _____
   _____.

   This is important because _____
   _____.

4. Do you think being sent to prison is an appropriate punishment for all crimes? Why or why not?

   I feel that _____
   _____.

   To explain more clearly, _____
   _____.

5. What are some alternative forms of punishment to sending criminals to jail?

   My belief is _____
   _____.

   For example, _____
   _____.

Opinion Examples

Look at the opinion examples about the motion below and answer the questions.

Motion: Prisons are an ineffective form of punishment for criminals.

Opinion A Track 20

Prisons simply do not work. More than half of all criminals end up back in prison. The main reason for this is that spending time in jail does not treat the cause of criminal behavior. The only thing prisons do is make criminals become tougher and more violent. They do not teach inmates job skills. Rather than sending lawbreakers to prison, we should send them to rehabilitation clinics. Give them therapy to help them treat their problems and education to help them get proper jobs. This is the best solution to deal with lawbreakers.

Opinion B Track 21

There are some people who believe sending criminals to school will stop people from breaking the law. The problem is that a lot of criminals are dangerous people who need serious punishment. This is why we need prisons in our society. Newspapers report that prisons are too crowded, but this just means the police are doing their job properly. Currently, the United States has almost 220,000 prison inmates. These dangerous criminals are safely locked away from the rest of society. Of course, prisons are depressing places. They need to be so that criminals will regret their actions and never want to break the law again.

1. Underline the main idea of each opinion.

2. Which opinion is for the topic? Which one is against it?
    - FOR: _____
    - AGAINST: _____

3. What supporting ideas does each opinion give?
    - Opinion A: _____
    - Opinion B: _____

4. Create one more supporting idea for each argument.
    - Opinion A: _____
    - Opinion B: _____

Skills for Debate

Read and learn how to create your examples.

How Should You Create Your Examples?

After presenting your supporting reasons, the next step in a debate is to give your supporting examples. Examples are different from supporting reasons because they describe **specific facts**, **situations**, and **events**. Like the supporting reasons, your examples must be **clearly related** to your arguments. Strong examples **prove** why your argument is **true**. Examples that are not obviously related to your argument or do not have enough detail can actually weaken your argument, so be sure to create good examples.

Practicing Debate Skills

Read the following debate topic and its supporting arguments. Analyze the examples given for each argument and decide if they are strong or weak. If they are strong, explain why. If they are weak, rewrite them to make them stronger.

Sample Motion: Schools should use physical punishment to discipline children.

1 Argument: Using physical punishment puts teachers in a position of authority.

Example: Schools have used physical punishment for hundreds of years. School punishment by caning was very common in Britain during the 19th and 20th centuries. With such a long tradition, there is no reason to stop using physical punishment.

(☐ STRONG   ☐ WEAK)

→ _____

2 Argument: Corporal punishment is a quick way to punish students effectively.

Example: School Principal David Nixon once said, "As soon as the student has been punished, he can go back to his class and continue learning, in contrast to out-of-school suspension, which removes him from the educational process and gives him a free 'holiday.'"

(☐ STRONG   ☐ WEAK)

→ _____

Unit 07 B Debating the Topic

Creating Your Debate

Motion: Prisons are an ineffective form of punishment for criminals.

What are your arguments? Get into two groups and plan for the debate. Decide whether your team is FOR (agree) or AGAINST (disagree) the motion. Then, create your ARE: Argument, Reason, and Example. Use the example arguments below and the research from your workbook to help create your arguments.

■ Example Arguments

FOR	AGAINST
Argument	**Argument**
Prisons do not work because they do not help inmates correct their problems.	Life in prison is difficult and dangerous, and this discourages people from breaking the law.
Reason	**Reason**
When people are sent to prison, they spend most of their days in their prison cell. They are usually not allowed to study or take classes. This is a waste of time, and it also does not teach prisoners how to become productive citizens.	At any time in prison, there could be fights and other acts of violence. This frightening environment makes inmates never want to return to prison.
Example	**Example**
Less than 1 percent of prisoners who receive a college degree during their prison sentence return to prison.	In one documentary about prisons, a prisoner commented that prison was "the most terrible place on Earth." He said that he would make sure he never breaks the law again so that he does not have to go back to prison.

■ Arguments FOR/AGAINST the Motion

ARGUMENT 1

Argument

_____
_____
_____
_____
_____

Reason

_____
_____
_____
_____
_____

Example

_____
_____
_____
_____
_____
_____

ARGUMENT 2

Argument

_____
_____
_____
_____
_____

Reason

_____
_____
_____
_____
_____

Example

_____
_____
_____
_____
_____
_____

ARGUMENT 3

Argument

_____
_____
_____
_____
_____

Reason

_____
_____
_____
_____
_____

Example

_____
_____
_____
_____
_____
_____

Actual Debate

Now, it's time to debate. Use the flow chart below to help you organize the debate.
The introductory expressions have been provided to help you. Put your arguments in logical order and make clear rebuttals to the opposing team's arguments.

Agree Opening Statement
We, the members of the pro team, believe that _____.

Agree Argument 1
For our first argument, we believe _____
_____
_____
_____.

Rebuttal 1
Your team's claim that _____
_____ is incorrect because _____.

Agree Argument 2
Second, it is undeniable that _____
_____.

Rebuttal 2
Even though _____
_____,
we must point out that _____
_____.

Agree Argument 3
Our final argument is _____
_____.

Agree Closing Statement
On the whole, our team contends that _____
_____.

Disagree Opening Statement
We disagree with the idea that _____
_____.

Rebuttal 1
You claimed that _____
_____. However, _____
_____.

Disagree Argument 1
As for our first argument, _____
_____.

Rebuttal 2
Your team wrongly claims that _____
_____.

Disagree Argument 2
In addition, we believe that _____
_____
_____.

Rebuttal 3
In spite of your argument that _____
_____,
we believe _____.

Disagree Argument 3
The last point we would like to make against this topic is _____
_____.

Disagree Closing Statement
Our overall opinion is that _____
_____.

Sum Up the Debate

Finish the debate summary.

AGREEING SIDE'S ARGUMENT

The debate topic for today was _____.

The agreeing team claimed that _____.

For their opening argument, they said _____.

To support this, they explained that _____
_____.

Second, they posited that _____

They specifically mentioned _____
_____.

Their final argument was _____.

In detail, they explained that _____
_____.

DISAGREEING SIDE'S ARGUMENT

The con team presented a different opinion _____
_____.

To start with, they claimed that _____.

They mentioned _____
_____ to support their claim.

Next, they argued that _____.

Their supporting idea was _____
_____.

For their last argument, they contended _____.

They gave the example of _____
_____.

Unit 08 Cosmetic Plastic Surgery

A. Discuss the following questions as a class.
1. What do you see in the picture above?
2. How does the woman's face in the left side of the picture look different from the right side?
3. Why do you think the woman changed the way her face looks?

B. Answer the following questions with a partner.
1. Do you know anyone who has gotten plastic surgery? If so, who?
2. Why do you think people get plastic surgery?
3. Is it okay for people to change the way they look, or should they just accept their natural appearance?

Unit 08 A Learning about the Topic

Should people be allowed to get plastic surgery for cosmetic purposes?

Read the passage and underline the main ideas. Track 22

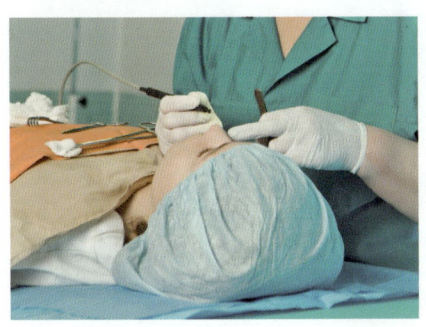

South Korea has the highest rate of plastic surgery in the world. In a small number of these cases, plastic surgery is necessary, such as reconstructive surgery after an accident. However, most of the time, South Koreans get platic surgery only for cosmetic purposes. There are many who claim that **elective** plastic surgery is dangerous and should be banned. Other people argue that plastic surgery is a practical way for people to improve their appearance and to feel better about themselves.

The main reason plastic surgery is so popular is that it is widely available. Because it is easy to get plastic surgery, many people feel **compelled** to get it. If there were fewer plastic surgery clinics, then fewer people would have surgery done. Plastic surgery has social **implications** as well. Plastic surgery procedures are fairly expensive. They generally cost between $2,000 and $10,000. Allowing plastic surgery to continue will create social divisions. There will be those people who can afford surgery and those who cannot. Lastly, some evidence suggests that plastic surgery can increase the chance of health problems occurring. In one study, women who had plastic surgery were 21 percent more likely to get cancer than women who did not.

While there are certainly drawbacks to plastic surgery, banning it would not be so straightforward. History has shown that banning an activity will not stop people from doing it. This has happened with drugs and alcohol. If plastic surgery were banned, people would still have it done. The difference is that the government would not **regulate** the procedures. This would make them more dangerous. Another point is that governments do not have the right to tell people what they may do with their bodies. People who want to have surgery to improve their appearance should be allowed to do so. Likewise, plastic surgery is popular because there is a high **demand** for it. Many people want to improve their appearance. Otherwise, all the plastic surgery clinics would already be out of business.

Vocabulary Check

Choose the correct word for each definition.

> elective   compelled   implication   regulate   demand

1 to make rules or laws that control something   _____
2 the need or desire to buy goods or services   _____
3 a possible future effect or result   _____
4 done or taken by choice; not medically necessary   _____
5 made or forced to do something   _____

Comprehension Questions

Check the correct answer for each question.

1 In which case is plastic surgery necessary?
- ☐ Having reconstructive surgery after an accident
- ☐ Having surgery done only for cosmetic purposes

2 Why might plastic surgery create social divisions?
- ☐ Because not everybody is able to afford plastic surgery procedures
- ☐ Because there are a high number of plastic surgery clinics

3 What would happen if the government banned plastic surgery?
- ☐ People would no longer get plastic surgery.
- ☐ Plastic surgery would not be regulated and would be more dangerous.

4 How do people benefit from plastic surgery?
- ☐ They can improve their appearance and feel better about themselves.
- ☐ They can impress more people and get higher-paying jobs.

Questions for Debate

Think of and share ideas to explore the debatable issues in the article. Be sure to state your opinion clearly and to provide one supporting idea for each opinion.

1. What are some of the main reasons you think people get plastic surgery?

   It is my opinion that _____
   _____.

   To go into more detail, _____
   _____.

2. Is it fair to judge people by their looks? Why or why not?

   My feeling is that _____
   _____.

   The reason I feel this way is _____
   _____.

3. Should the government be allowed to control what people do to their own bodies? Explain.

   I think that _____
   _____.

   For example, _____
   _____.

4. How can getting plastic surgery help people be more successful in their work?

   To me, it seems that _____
   _____.

   To give you a better idea, consider that _____
   _____.

5. What do you think would happen if the prices of plastic surgery procedures were increased?

   What I think would happen is _____
   _____.

   Let me clarify this by saying that _____
   _____.

Opinion Examples

Look at the opinion examples about the motion below and answer the questions.

Motion: Elective plastic surgery is beneficial for people and society.

Opinion A Track 23

Elective plastic surgery is a dangerous practice that must be stopped right away. For one, plastic surgery can lead to health problems. Plastic surgery procedures can have dangerous side effects. One woman got surgery to make her jaw slimmer. After the surgery, she was not able to close her mouth fully. Plastic surgery can also increase a person's chances of getting cancer. Why should the government allow people to get cosmetic surgery that could end their lives? The popularity of plastic surgery also encourages people to focus too much on physical appearance. We should not judge people by how they look but by the content of their character.

Opinion B Track 24

Once again, the government wants to put too many controls on the lives of the people. The government should allow people to get plastic surgery procedures if they want to. A small number of people suffer medical problems because of plastic surgery. But for most people, getting plastic surgery is a great experience. If the government were to ban plastic surgery because it is slightly dangerous, it would have to ban almost every other activity we do. In addition, the reality is that our society greatly values appearance. If people make themselves look better, they can be more successful in their careers and personal lives.

1 Underline the main idea of each opinion.

2 Which opinion is for the topic? Which one is against it?
   - FOR: _____
   - AGAINST: _____

3 What supporting ideas does each opinion give?
   - Opinion A: _____
   - Opinion B: _____

4 Create one more supporting idea for each argument.
   - Opinion A: _____
   - Opinion B: _____

Skills for Debate

Read and learn how to introduce your points clearly.

How Should You Create Your Examples?

You should use many different types of examples to support your debate. Two of the most common types of examples are **personal experience** and **common sense**. Personal experience is where you describe something related to the topic that you or someone else has done. Common sense examples are where you describe a widely known fact that proves your argument. More effective example types are **expert opinions** and **statistics**. In an expert opinion, you mention information created by a professional in the field of the topic. Statistics are facts that use numbers to explain facts and ideas.

Practicing Debate Skills

Read each of the following arguments below. Then, create examples for the different types of examples listed. Some phrases have been given to help you.

> **Sample Motion:** Companies should not be allowed to hire employees based on appearance.

1 Argument: Employers are more impressed by people with a good appearance.

① **Personal Experience:** Let me share the experience of _____

_____

_____

② **Statistic:** According to statistics, _____

_____

_____

2 Argument: Many jobs require workers to have a certain appearance.

① **Common Sense:** For instance, _____

_____

_____

② **Expert Opinion:** According to psychologist Gordon Patzer, _____

_____

_____

93

Unit 08 B Debating the Topic

Creating Your Debate

Motion: Elective plastic surgery is beneficial for people and society.

What are your arguments? Get into two groups and plan for the debate. Decide whether your team is FOR (agree) or AGAINST (disagree) the motion. Then, create your ARE: Argument, Reason, and Example. Use the example arguments below and the research from your workbook to help create your arguments.

■ Example Arguments

FOR	AGAINST
Argument	**Argument**
Banning plastic surgery will not stop people from having procedures done.	Allowing plastic surgery makes people concentrate too much on physical appearance.
Reason	**Reason**
People will still do an activity if they really want to do it even if it is banned. The problem is that banned activities will not be regulated and will therefore more dangerous.	People often get plastic surgery because they are unhappy about themselves in some way. While getting plastic surgery may improve their feelings for a while, it does not make them permanently happy.
Example	**Example**
In 1919, the United States made it illegal to purchase alcohol. The overall number of people who drank alcohol slightly decreased, but millions of people still drank alcohol illegally. If plastic surgery were made illegal, a similar situation would occur.	A study conducted by the British Association of Plastic Surgeons did not find a major change in the self-esteem levels of people who had plastic surgery.

Arguments FOR/AGAINST the Motion

ARGUMENT 1

Argument

_____
_____
_____
_____
_____

Reason

_____
_____
_____
_____
_____

Example

_____
_____
_____
_____
_____
_____

ARGUMENT 2

Argument

_____
_____
_____
_____
_____

Reason

_____
_____
_____
_____
_____

Example

_____
_____
_____
_____
_____
_____

ARGUMENT 3

Argument

_____
_____
_____
_____
_____

Reason

_____
_____
_____
_____
_____

Example

_____
_____
_____
_____
_____
_____

Actual Debate

Now, it's time to debate. Use the flow chart below to help you organize the debate.
The introductory expressions have been provided to help you. Put your arguments in logical order and make clear rebuttals to the opposing team's arguments.

Agree Opening Statement
It is our team's opinion that _____
_____.

Disagree Opening Statement
We disagree with the pro team that _____
_____.

Agree Argument 1
First of all, _____
_____
_____
_____
_____.

Rebuttal 1
Your team claims that _____
_____. However,
_____
_____.

Disagree Argument 1
To give our first argument, _____
_____.

Rebuttal 1
While the con team claims _____
_____, we feel that
_____
_____.

Rebuttal 2
Your team wrongly claims that _____
_____
_____
_____.

Agree Argument 2
Next, we believe that _____
_____
_____.

Disagree Argument 2
In addition, we believe that _____
_____
_____.

Rebuttal 2
You said that _____
_____
_____.

Even so, _____
_____.

Rebuttal 3
Our opponents claim _____
_____
_____.

The truth of the matter is _____
_____.

Agree Argument 3
Finally, we must point out that _____
_____
_____.

Disagree Argument 3
For our final point, we would like to explain
_____
_____.

Agree Closing Statement
In summary, our team holds that _____
_____.

Disagree Closing Statement
In conclusion, we disagree that _____
_____.

Sum Up the Debate

Finish the debate summary.

AGREEING SIDE'S ARGUMENT

The debate motion for today was _____.

The pro team started off by arguing that _____.

For their opening argument, they mentioned _____.

The reasoning was _____
_____.

For their second idea, the pro team argued that _____

For example, _____
_____.

Finally, they reasoned that _____

For instance, _____
_____.

DISAGREEING SIDE'S ARGUMENT

The con team felt differently. They claimed that _____
_____.

For their first argument, they said that _____

Specifically, they mentioned that _____
_____.

Their second reason was that _____

For instance, _____
_____.

Finally, they explained that _____

They illustrated this by mentioning that _____
_____.

97

Chapter 5

Doing Research

Unit 09 Physical Education in Schools

Unit 10 Space Exploration

Unit 09 Physical Education in Schools

A. Discuss the following questions as a class.
1. What do you see in the picture above?
2. Are all of the students in the picture enjoying themselves? Explain.
3. What do you think happened to the boy lying on the ground?

B. Answer the following questions with a partner.
1. Do you enjoy physical education class in school? Why or why not?
2. What can students learn from having physical education classes?
3. How can students be harmed because of physical education classes?

Unit 09 A Learning about the Topic

Should all students be required to take physical education classes?

Read the passage and underline the main ideas. Track 25

For some students, physical education (PE) class can be the most exciting part of school. For other students, it is a nightmare. Just like students, parents, teachers, and school districts are **divided** about physical education. Some districts have been cutting PE classes in order to save money. Others contend that exercise education is necessary to reduce student obesity rates. We must consider both sides of the issue before reaching a decision.

Many students simply do not wish to participate in physical education classes. Large numbers of students come to school with "sick notes." They do this so that they may be excused from PE class. For these students, physical education is a **burden**, not a benefit. Part of the reason for this is that many students are not talented at sports. Sports is a specialized subject, just like music. In many schools, students can choose to take music if they want to. The same rule should apply to PE classes. Offering physical education can also be **costly** for schools. Schools need to have large gymnasiums and lots of sports equipment. A significant amount of schools are underfunded. Schools must use their money to provide quality academic instruction.

To help students stay healthy, requiring PE classes is the obvious solution. These days, most young people spend lots of time indoors. Their primary source of physical activity is PE class. With all the health benefits of exercise, it is logical to require physical education. Many PE classes also teach students about dieting and healthy eating. Due to this, physical education can promote healthier lifestyles among all students. This leads to having a healthier society. However, the benefits of PE class **extend** beyond physical exercise. Physical education allows students to learn about themselves and their abilities. Not everybody is academic. Some students are more talented at physical activities. Without **mandatory** physical education, millions of potential athletes would be denied the chance to discover their talents.

Vocabulary Check

Choose the correct word for each definition.

| divided | burden | costly | extend | mandatory |

1 to go farther or beyond _____
2 something difficult that you must do _____
3 having a high price; expensive _____
4 separated by different opinions _____
5 required by rule or law _____

Comprehension Questions

Check the correct answer for each question.

1 Why is physical education class a burden for some students?
- ☐ Because sports is a specialized subject
- ☐ Because they are not talented at sports

2 What do schools need to spend money on to have PE classes?
- ☐ Large gymnasiums and sports equipment
- ☐ Sports fields and academic instruction

3 How does requiring PE class lead to a healthier society?
- ☐ It encourages students to join athletic teams.
- ☐ It promotes healthier lifestyles among students.

4 What is true about students talented at physical activities?
- ☐ They can discover their talents through PE class.
- ☐ They can develop their skills in various sports.

Questions for Debate

Think of and share ideas to explore the debatable issues in the article. Be sure to state your opinion clearly and to provide one supporting idea for each opinion.

1 Schools require students to take many different academic classes. Do you think schools have a right to require students to exercise? Explain.

My feeling about this is _____
_____.

I have this opinion because _____
_____.

2 What are some reasons that some students dislike PE class?

I believe that _____
_____.

For example, _____
_____.

3 Is it more important for students to get physical exercise or to learn about healthy eating habits?

It seems to me that _____
_____.

To go into detail, _____
_____.

4 What are some potential dangers or accidents that could occur because of PE class?

My thoughts are that _____
_____.

To give an example, _____
_____.

5 If students do not want to take PE class, what other classes should they take instead?

What I think they should do is _____
_____.

Let me explain this by mentioning that _____
_____.

103

Opinion Examples

Look at the opinion examples about the motion below and answer the questions.

Motion: Students should not be required to take physical education classes.

Opinion A Track 26

It is my opinion that physical education class should be optional for students. Not all students are good at sports. They aren't interested in them at all. This is how I feel. I always dread going to PE class. The other students never want me to play on their team, so I always get picked last. That makes me embarrassed and sad. Plus, when I'm outside running around, I get hot and sweaty. For the rest of the school day, I feel sticky and uncomfortable. I wish that students could take other classes instead of PE, like community service classes or band classes.

Opinion B Track 27

Some students may not like taking PE class, but that doesn't mean schools should stop requiring PE class. Physical education class should be mandatory for all students. There are many things in life that aren't enjoyable, but we should do them anyway. For example, a lot of people don't like spinach, but they eat it anyway because it's healthy. Students need to learn that we can't only do what we want. PE class also has important health benefits for students. Let's face it. A lot of students get little exercise these days. If gym class were optional, then millions of students would get no exercise at all.

1 Underline the main idea of each opinion.

2 Which opinion is for the topic? Which one is against it?
- FOR: _____
- AGAINST: _____

3 What supporting ideas does each opinion give?
- Opinion A: _____
- Opinion B: _____

4 Create one more supporting idea for each argument.
- Opinion A: _____
- Opinion B: _____

Skills for Debate

Read and learn how to do your research.

How Should You Do Your Research?

When creating your examples for debate, it is a good idea to do research. The best ways to do research are through **online search engines** such as Google and **online encyclopedias** such as Wikipedia. However, to find the information you want, you must learn how to choose **key terms** that will give you the best search results. Key terms include the specific **nouns** and **verbs** related to your argument. You can also use **adjectives** and **comparative adjectives** such as "more" and "most." Finally, you should add the terms "statistics," "percentage," "expert opinion," "academic study," or "personal experience" to make your research more specific.

Practicing Debate Skills

Think of the best key terms for researching each of the arguments below. Make sure that your key words are appropriate for each type of example. Some words have been provided to help you.

1. Many schools do not have enough money to fund physical education classes. (**Statistics**)
   - Key Words: public schools, funding, _____

2. Physical education classes give students the exercise they need to stay healthy. (**Personal Experience**)
   - Key Words: health benefits, going to school, _____

3. A number of students can be bullied or made fun of during PE class. (**Common Sense**)
   - Key Words: physical education class, overweight students, _____

4. Students who get more exercise get higher grades on average. (**Expert Opinion**)
   - Key Words: boost, test scores, _____

Unit 09 B Debating the Topic

Creating Your Debate

Motion: Students should not be required to take physical education classes.

What are your arguments? Get into two groups and plan for the debate. Decide whether your team is FOR (agree) or AGAINST (disagree) the motion. Then, create your ARE: Argument, Reason, and Example. Use the example arguments below and the research from your workbook to help create your arguments.

■ Example Arguments

FOR	AGAINST
Argument	**Argument**
Students who dislike PE class can take other classes that are more beneficial for them.	Schools require students to take a variety of classes to prepare them for the future.
Reason	**Reason**
For students who are not athletic, physical education class is a waste of time. It would be better for these students to take other classes where they can do work that interests them more.	Students are required to take math, language, and science classes. The reason is that these classes give students the skills and knowledge they need to succeed. PE class is no different.
Example	**Example**
In some schools, students are allowed to be exempt from PE class if they pass a physical fitness test. Other schools allow students to skip PE class and do community service or be in the school's band instead.	Over 95 percent of high schools in the United States require students to take physical education classes. This is done to make sure that all students do the physical activity they need to stay healthy.

Arguments FOR/AGAINST the Motion

ARGUMENT 1	ARGUMENT 2	ARGUMENT 3
Argument	**Argument**	**Argument**
Reason	**Reason**	**Reason**
Example	**Example**	**Example**

Actual Debate

Now, it's time to debate. Use the flow chart below to help you organize the debate.
The introductory expressions have been provided to help you. Put your arguments in logical order and make clear rebuttals to the opposing team's arguments.

Agree Opening Statement
Today, we will explain why _____.

Agree Argument 1
For our opening argument, _____
_____
_____
_____.

Rebuttal 1
In spite of your claim that _____
_____, we believe that _____
_____.

Agree Argument 2
For our second argument, consider that _____
_____.

Rebuttal 2
Our team is against the idea that _____
_____.

Agree Argument 3
Our final argument is _____
_____.

Agree Closing Statement
Overall, our team contends that _____
_____.

Disagree Opening Statement
Unlike the opposing team, we feel that _____
_____.

Rebuttal 1
You believe that _____
_____.

This is incorrect because _____
_____.

Disagree Argument 1
Our first argument is that _____
_____.

Rebuttal 2
It is wrong to assume that _____
_____.

Disagree Argument 2
It is also necessary to keep in mind that _____
_____.

Rebuttal 3
While the pro side feels _____
_____, we feel that _____
_____.

Disagree Argument 3
Lastly, it must be mentioned that _____
_____.

Disagree Closing Statement
In conclusion, we disagree that _____
_____.

Sum Up the Debate

Finish the debate summary.

AGREEING SIDE'S ARGUMENT

Today's debate motion was _____.

The pro team argued _____.

Their first argument was _____.

They supported this by explaining that _____
_____.

Next, they explained _____

In more detail, _____
_____.

Their final reason was _____.

Specifically, _____
_____.

DISAGREEING SIDE'S ARGUMENT

The second team argued differently. They felt _____
_____.

Their opening argument was _____.

Their supporting idea was _____
_____.

For their second argument, they presented _____

To be specific, _____
_____.

The con team's final argument was _____.

For their example, they said _____
_____.

Unit 10 Space Exploration

A. Discuss the following questions as a class.
1. What do you see in the picture above?
2. What do astronauts do when they travel into outer space?
3. How can space exploration benefit the lives of people on the Earth?

B. Answer the following questions with a partner.
1. Do you think space exploration is necessary? Why or why not?
2. What are some inventions that space travel helped to create?
3. What are some other ways the money for space exploration could be used?

Unit 10 A Learning about the Topic

Should governments spend time and money exploring outer space?

Read the passage and underline the main ideas.   Track 28

In 1957, the Soviet Union became the first nation to reach outer space with its satellite *Sputnik*. Following this, the United States and Soviet Union began a "space race" that lasted for nearly two decades. Since the end of the Cold War in the 1980s, the future of space exploration has become less clear. Today, the Earth is reaching its limits for population growth. It may be time for humanity to turn its attention to outer space once again.

The advantages of space exploration programs are numerous. For one, space exploration has improved our daily lives. It has led to the creation of technology that people use all the time. One example is the central processing unit (CPU), which is found in **countless** computer technologies today. Another example is the satellites that have made it possible for us to use cell phones. Additionally, space exploration can help society develop. To go into outer space, a country needs highly trained scientists and advanced technology. Space exploration **facilitates** the development of advanced knowledge. A final benefit of space exploration is that it pushes the **boundaries** of human knowledge. Humans are naturally curious. Exploring outer space satisfies our need to learn more about the world and the universe.

Opponents of the space race have just as many arguments supporting their opinion. First, space exploration requires a lot of money. This money could be spent on more **pressing** issues. Our world is faced with war, poverty, disease, and hunger. Exploring space does little to help solve these problems. Similarly, the results of space exploration do not justify its high cost. The scientific community benefits from experiments conducted in outer space, but most people do not. Instead of spending several billion dollars building a space shuttle, the money could be used for more practical research. The third point is that space exploration promotes nationalistic competition. The United States and the Soviet Union used the space race to **outdo** one another. In today's globalized society, such nationalistic competition would do more harm than good.

Vocabulary Check

Choose the correct word for each definition.

| countless | facilitate | boundary | pressing | outdo |

1 to do better than someone else _____
2 to make something easier to do _____
3 a point where something ends and another begins _____
4 too much in number to count _____
5 very important and needing immediate attention _____

Comprehension Questions

Check the correct answer for each question.

1 Which nation was the first to reach outer space?
   ☐ The United States
   ☐ The Soviet Union

2 How has space exploration improved our daily lives?
   ☐ It has led to the creation of CPUs and satellites.
   ☐ It helped scientists design new types of cell phones.

3 What does a country need to go into outer space?
   ☐ A lot of money and advanced technology
   ☐ A large scientific community and practical research

4 What are some other issues the money spent on space exploration could be used on? Choose TWO correct answers.
   ☐ poverty   ☐ weapons
   ☐ schools   ☐ diseases

Questions for Debate

Think of and share ideas to explore the debatable issues in the article. Be sure to state your opinion clearly and to provide one supporting idea for each opinion.

1. Are the problems we face on the Earth more important than issues in outer space? Explain.

   It is my belief that _____
   _____.

   For example, _____
   _____.

2. Besides technological benefits, what are some other advantages of space exploration programs?

   Some other advantages are _____
   _____.

   For instance, _____
   _____.

3. Do you think humanity will ever need to leave the Earth? If so, what role could space exploration have?

   In my opinion, _____
   _____.

   To be more specific, _____
   _____.

4. The U.S. spends less than 0.5 percent of its annual budget on space exploration. Is this too much or too little to spend?

   My feeling is that _____
   _____.

   I believe that because _____
   _____.

5. How important are science and technology to the future of our society?

   I think that _____
   _____.

   For instance, _____
   _____.

113

Opinion Examples

Look at the opinion examples about the motion below and answer the questions.

Motion: Space exploration is important for humanity and must continue.

Opinion A Track 29

When I was younger, I dreamed of going into outer space. Now, however, I realize that exploring outer space is a waste of time. Astronauts conduct experiments in space, but most of them are not very practical. Knowing how plants grow in outer space doesn't really improve life on the Earth. Sure, there have been some developments such as the CPU. Yet scientists could have just as easily developed these on the Earth. Space exploration also takes budget money away from more urgent problems on the Earth. Governments could use the money spent on space exploration for education or poverty. That would be a better use of the money.

Opinion B Track 30

While space exploration may not always be practical, it is necessary for humanity to continue to develop. The most obvious benefit of space exploration is the development of science and technology. The rocket technology used in space exploration has been adapted for use in jet planes. This has allowed millions of people to travel across the world easily. Plus, there's the fact that space exploration increases our knowledge of the rest of the universe. Our planet is just one tiny part of the universe. Someday, we may need to move to other parts of the galaxy. Space exploration will make this possible.

1. Underline the main idea of each opinion.

2. Which opinion is for the topic? Which one is against it?
   - FOR: _____
   - AGAINST: _____

3. What supporting ideas does each opinion give?
   - Opinion A: _____
   - Opinion B: _____

4. Create one more supporting idea for each argument.
   - Opinion A: _____
   - Opinion B: _____

Skills for Debate

Read and learn how to do your research.

How Should You Do Your Research?

When doing research online, there are many different types of sources you can use. Some are **reliable sources**. These are sources that are most likely to be well-written with good information you can use in your debate. Websites run by news organizations, universities, and governments are usually reliable. **Unreliable sources**, on the other hand, often contain untrue or inaccurate information. These are sources that are created by private individuals. These people may not have a very good understanding of the topic you are researching. So, when you are doing your research, make sure to use only reliable sources.

Practicing Debate Skills

Read the list of research sources below. Then, decide whether they are RELIABLE or UNRELIABLE research resources.

1. A blog written by a student
2. A research site written by a professor
3. A debate site that anyone can add information to
4. An article from a major newspaper
5. A website where students post their homework
6. Statistics created by a government organization
7. A news magazine editorial
8. A story from an international news channel
9. A newsletter written by fans
10. A forum where users post opinions about news

RELIABLE Sources
- _____
- _____
- _____
- _____
- _____

UNRELIABLE Sources
- _____
- _____
- _____
- _____
- _____

Unit 10 B Debating the Topic

Creating Your Debate

Motion: Space exploration is important for humanity and must continue.

What are your arguments? Get into two groups and plan for the debate. Decide whether your team is FOR (agree) or AGAINST (disagree) the motion. Then, create your ARE: Argument, Reason, and Example. Use the example arguments below and the research from your workbook to help create your arguments.

- **Example Arguments**

FOR	AGAINST
Argument	**Argument**
Space exploration allows scientists to develop new technology.	The money used for space exploration should be spent on other issues.
Reason	**Reason**
Space exploration gives scientists a specific goal to work toward. This helps them develop advanced technologies more quickly and efficiently.	Space exploration is a great idea, but there are too many problems on the Earth that need to be solved. Each day, millions of people starve to death or die in wars. Space exploration money could be better used for these issues.
Example	**Example**
The CPU was developed because scientists needed to find a way to use computers in outer space. The CPU might have taken much longer to develop without space exploration.	The amount spent on space exploration by the U.S. government is the same amount spent on education each year. Yet education is far more important for the future of humanity.

■ Arguments FOR/AGAINST the Motion

ARGUMENT 1	ARGUMENT 2	ARGUMENT 3
Argument	**Argument**	**Argument**
Reason	**Reason**	**Reason**
Example	**Example**	**Example**

Actual Debate

Now, it's time to debate. Use the flow chart below to help you organize the debate.
The introductory expressions have been provided to help you. Put your arguments in logical order and make clear rebuttals to the opposing team's arguments.

Agree Opening Statement
We, the members of the pro team, believe that _____ is beneficial.

Disagree Opening Statement
Unlike the pro team, we feel that _____.

Agree Argument 1
First of all, _____.

Rebuttal 1
Your team claims that _____.

However, _____.

Disagree Argument 1
To give our first argument, _____.

Rebuttal 1
Your team claims that _____, yet _____.

Agree Argument 2
We also support this motion because _____.

Rebuttal 2
It is wrong to assume that _____

because _____.

Disagree Argument 2
It is also necessary to consider that _____.

Rebuttal 2
Our team disagrees that _____.

Agree Argument 3
Our final argument is _____.

Rebuttal 3
The opposing team incorrectly believes that _____.

Disagree Argument 3
Lastly, it should be mentioned that _____.

Agree Closing Statement
To conclude, the pro team believes that _____.

Disagree Closing Statement
In sum, we disagree that _____.

Sum Up the Debate

Finish the debate summary.

AGREEING SIDE'S ARGUMENT

Our debate topic was _____.

The agreeing team's opinion was _____.

For their opening argument, they said _____.

To support this, they explained that _____

_____.

Next, the team posited _____.

Their claim was supported by _____

_____.

Finally, they reasoned _____.

For example, _____

_____.

DISAGREEING SIDE'S ARGUMENT

The con side presented the opposite opinion. They stated _____

_____.

To start with, they claimed that _____.

They mentioned _____

_____ to support their claim.

Their next argument was _____.

For intance, _____

_____.

Their final point was _____.

This was explained by _____

_____.

Instilling Knowledge and Skills
for Thoughtful Debate

DEBATE Pro

Book 2

Jonathan S. McClelland

Workbook

DARAKWON

DEBATE Pro
Book 2

Workbook

DARAKWON

Contents

How to Use This Book _4

Unit 01 Afterschool Academies _6

Unit 02 Genetically Modified Foods _10

Unit 03 Climate Change _14

Unit 04 Replacing Teachers with Computers _18

Unit 05 Using CCTVs in Public Places _22

Unit 06 Celebrity Salaries _26

Unit 07 Punishment for Criminals _30

Unit 08 Cosmetic Plastic Surgery _34

Unit 09 Physical Education in Schools _38

Unit 10 Space Exploration _42

How to Use This Book

Overview

The workbook is intended to supplement the main book both during class and for homework. It provides space for students to take notes during class and to do additional research outside of class.

Introduction for each section

Organizing Ideas

This part requires students to analyze the reading passage from the main book and write down each of the arguments and examples for and against the topic.

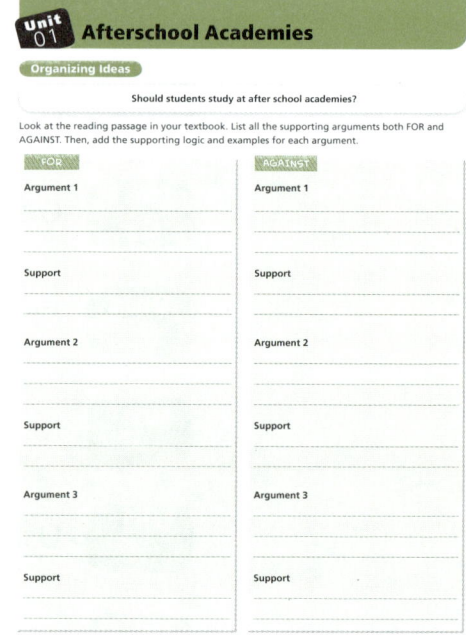

Making Supporting Examples

This section helps students develop their skills in making examples. In each book, five types of examples are explained: statistics, expert opinions, facts, academic studies, and personal opinions.

Additional Research

This section provides students with additional information about the topic based on the type of example explained in the previous section. The information is followed by four brief comprehension questions. Sample phrases are provided to help students create their answers.

Your Research

In this section, students are asked to do additional research outside of class. They are encouraged to find information from magazines, newspapers, or academic websites and to write or tape the material in the space provided. Based on the information they find, students are asked to create four additional examples which they can use during their debate.

Debate Note-Taking

This section provides space which students can use to take notes during the debate.

Peer Evaluation

This part requires students to evaluate their peers' debate performance. Eight criteria are provided along with a ten-point scale for each criterion with a total maximum score of eighty points for each student.

Unit 01 Afterschool Academies

Organizing Ideas

Should students study at after school academies?

Look at the reading passage in your textbook. List all the supporting arguments both FOR and AGAINST. Then, add the supporting logic and examples for each argument.

FOR	AGAINST
Argument 1	**Argument 1**
Support	**Support**
Argument 2	**Argument 2**
Support	**Support**
Argument 3	**Argument 3**
Support	**Support**

Making Supporting Examples: Personal Experience

Personal experience is your experience related to the topic. Using personal experience can be a good way to support your argument if you explain how your experience proves your point. However, you should be careful because one person's experience might not be common. This can actually weaken your argument. Below are some personal experiences related to the topic of afterschool academies.

Additional Research

Before starting your argument, let's do some extra research on the topic. Read the personal experiences about afterschool academies.

Hyejin Lee, a sixth grade student

To go to an international middle school next year, I must attend afterschool academies. Of course, I would sometimes rather stay at home and rest or play with my friends. But I need to stand out from other students when I apply to international middle schools this fall. For this reason, my mother has enrolled me in many afterschool academies. The most important ones for me are my English and math academies because I need to excel at these subjects to get into an international school. If I just study these subjects at school, I won't develop enough skills and knowledge to get into the schools I want. So for me, afterschool academies are necessary for success.

Josh Choi, a seventh grade student

The time I spent in the United States changed my opinion about afterschool academies. I used to think that they were crucial for success in life, but now I'm not so sure. There are just so many important lessons kids learn by being outside a classroom. Kids in the United States study, but they also have fun and socialize with their friends after school. Before, I thought that this was a waste of time. But now I realize that some of the most important life lessons happen outside the classroom. Kids can learn how to interact well with others. They can also develop creativity and get plenty of exercise. Students in Korea learn a lot from afterschool academies, but they also give up many other learning opportunities because of them.

Work with a partner and answer the following questions. Phrases have been provided to help you.

1. Why does Hyejin think afterschool academies will help her get into an international middle school?

   → *She thinks that they will help her because* _____.

2. What does Hyejin believe about only studying English and math at school?

   → *Her belief is* _____.

3. How are the lives of students in the United States different from the lives of students in Korea?

   → *Their lives are different in that* _____.

4. What are some skills students can learn by not attending afterschool academies?

   → *Students can learn* _____.

Your Research

Find an article about afterschool academies from a magazine, newspaper, or academic website. Paste or tape the article in your workbook in the space below.

Paste or Tape Your Research Article Here

Read your article and write four specific examples or pieces of evidence you can use for your debate. Try to include different types of examples, including opinion polls, statistics, academic studies, and general facts.

- _____
- _____
- _____
- _____

Debate Note-Taking

Use this page to take notes about the opposing team's arguments during the debate.

Note-Taking

_____
_____
_____
_____
_____
_____
_____
_____
_____
_____

Peer Evaluation

Read the assessment criteria and objectively evaluate your peers on a scale from 1 to 10.

CRITERIA	Name				
Understands the subject well	/10	/10	/10	/10	/10
Supports opinion with clear logic and examples	/10	/10	/10	/10	/10
Introduces opinions with appropriate connectors (In my view, I agree, For example, etc.)	/10	/10	/10	/10	/10
Uses a variety of vocabulary and expressions	/10	/10	/10	/10	/10
Accurately uses a variety of grammatical structures	/10	/10	/10	/10	/10
Does not monopolize the conversation and lets other people express themselves	/10	/10	/10	/10	/10
Listens attentively and respects other people's opinions	/10	/10	/10	/10	/10
Is able to accept criticism without becoming upset	/10	/10	/10	/10	/10
TOTAL SCORE	/80	/80	/80	/80	/80

Unit 02 Genetically Modified Foods

Organizing Ideas

Should scientists be allowed to modify the foods we eat?

Look at the reading passage in your textbook. List all the supporting arguments both FOR and AGAINST. Then, add the supporting logic and examples for each argument.

FOR

Argument 1
_____
_____
_____

Support
_____
_____
_____

Argument 2
_____
_____
_____

Support
_____
_____
_____

Argument 3
_____
_____
_____

Support
_____
_____
_____

AGAINST

Argument 1
_____
_____
_____

Support
_____
_____
_____

Argument 2
_____
_____
_____

Support
_____
_____
_____

Argument 3
_____
_____
_____

Support
_____
_____
_____

Making Supporting Examples: Academic Studies

Academic studies are research that is done by universities, governments, and large research organizations. During these studies, researchers examine events to understand what causes them and why they are important. Using academic studies is a good way to strengthen your argument. Below are some academic studies related to the topic of genetically modified foods.

Additional Research

Before starting your argument, let's do some extra research on the topic. Read the academic studies about genetically modified foods.

> For years, independent researchers were not allowed to study GM foods. This has made it difficult for scientists to know how GM foods can affect the body. After many years of trying, independent researchers were finally given permission to study the effects GM foods. Their findings suggest that GM foods are not yet safe enough to eat.
>
> **GM Foods Are Not Natural**
> In nature, only two closely related forms of life are able to breed. For instance, dogs breed with other dogs. Dogs don't breed with cats. However, GM foods are not developed naturally. They mix the genes from many different forms of life, such as bacteria, viruses, plants, and animals. This causes major changes to the DNA of crops. Major consequences can result, such as poor crop performance, damage to the environment, and allergic reactions.
>
> **GM Foods Are Not Safe to Eat**
> So far, there has only been one study on the safety of GM foods for humans. That study had a negative result. Studies of GM foods done on animals have had similar results. In several studies, animals have developed serious health problems after consuming GM foods. In one study, rats that ate GM tomatoes began to have stomach problems. GM peas caused allergic reactions in mice in another study. A different study with mice found that GM corn caused physical changes to various organs and the body's chemistry.

Work with a partner and answer the following questions. Phrases have been provided to help you.

1 Why was it difficult for scientists to know how GM foods affect the body?

→ *It was difficult for them to know because* _____.

2 How is the development of GM foods not natural?

→ *It is not natural since* _____.

3 What are some problems that can occur by changing the DNA of a crop?

→ *Some of the problems are* _____.

4 How did GM foods affect rats and mice in various studies?

→ *The rats and mice developed* _____,

   including _____.

Your Research

Find an article about genetically modified foods from a magazine, newspaper, or academic website. Paste or tape the article in your workbook in the space below.

Paste or Tape Your Research Article Here

Read your article and write four specific examples or pieces of evidence you can use for your debate. Try to include different types of examples, including opinion polls, statistics, academic studies, and general facts.

-
-
-
-

Debate Note-Taking

Use this page to take notes about the opposing team's arguments during the debate.

Note-Taking

_____
_____
_____
_____
_____
_____
_____
_____
_____
_____

Peer Evaluation

Read the assessment criteria and objectively evaluate your peers on a scale from 1 to 10.

CRITERIA	Name				
Understands the subject well	/10	/10	/10	/10	/10
Supports opinion with clear logic and examples	/10	/10	/10	/10	/10
Introduces opinions with appropriate connectors (In my view, I agree, For example, etc.)	/10	/10	/10	/10	/10
Uses a variety of vocabulary and expressions	/10	/10	/10	/10	/10
Accurately uses a variety of grammatical structures	/10	/10	/10	/10	/10
Does not monopolize the conversation and lets other people express themselves	/10	/10	/10	/10	/10
Listens attentively and respects other people's opinions	/10	/10	/10	/10	/10
Is able to accept criticism without becoming upset	/10	/10	/10	/10	/10
TOTAL SCORE	/80	/80	/80	/80	/80

Unit 03: Climate Change

Organizing Ideas

Should people worry about affecting the planet's climate?

Look at the reading passage in your textbook. List all the supporting arguments both FOR and AGAINST. Then, add the supporting logic and examples for each argument.

FOR	AGAINST
Argument 1	**Argument 1**
Support	**Support**
Argument 2	**Argument 2**
Support	**Support**
Argument 3	**Argument 3**
Support	**Support**

Making Supporting Examples: Statistics

Statistics are facts based on numbers. They are usually created by governments, universities, news organizations, and companies. Statistics often show the number of people, companies, and nations that agree with a certain opinion or policy. To show these numbers, statistics can include percentages, populations, and points. Below are some statistics related to the topic of climate change.

Additional Research

Before starting your argument, let's do some extra research on the topic. Read the statistics on climate change.

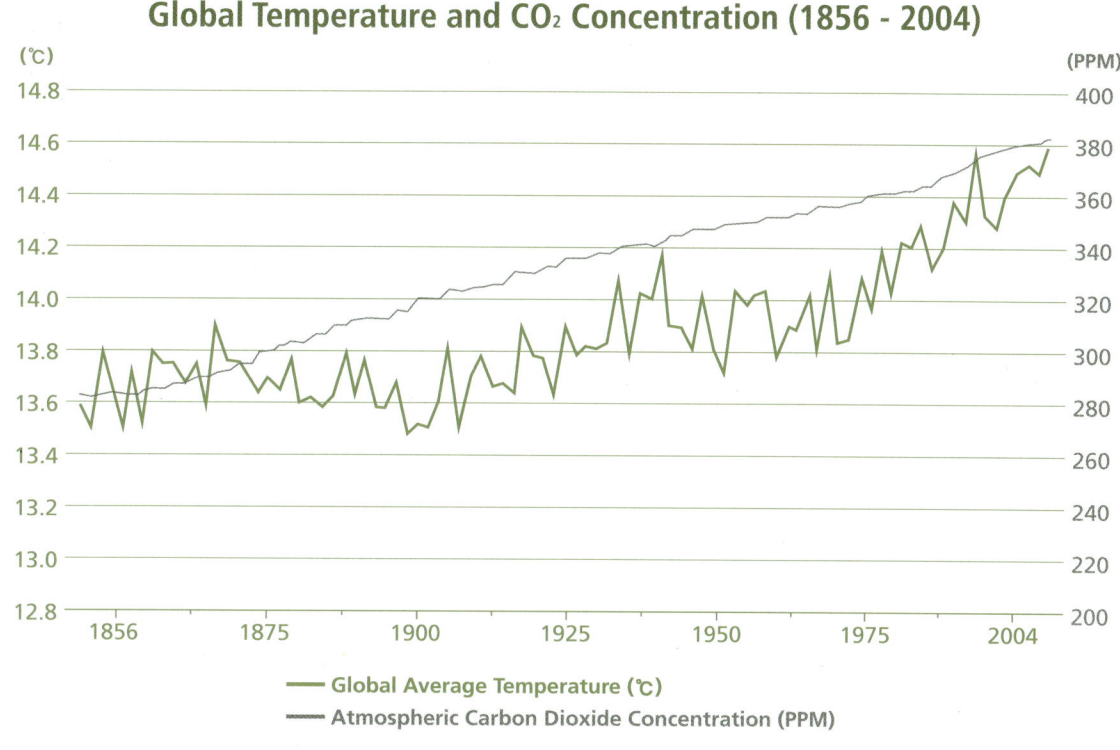

Global Temperature and CO_2 Concentration (1856 - 2004)

— Global Average Temperature (°C)
— Atmospheric Carbon Dioxide Concentration (PPM)

Work with a partner and answer the following questions. Phrases have been provided to help you.

1. By how many degrees did the global average temperature rise from 1856 to 2004?
   → The global average temperature changed by _____.

2. What is true about the atmospheric carbon dioxide concentration before and after 1925?
   → The atmospheric carbon dioxide concentration _____.

3. How did the global average temperature change in years when carbon dioxide levels were lower?
   → The average global temperature was _____.

4. What is the overall message of this graph?
   → The overall message of this graph is that _____.

Your Research

Find an article about climate change from a magazine, newspaper, or academic website. Paste or tape the article in your workbook in the space below.

Paste or Tape Your Research Article Here

Read your article and write four specific examples or pieces of evidence you can use for your debate. Try to include different types of examples, including opinion polls, statistics, academic studies, and general facts.

- _____
- _____
- _____
- _____

Debate Note-Taking

Use this page to take notes about the opposing team's arguments during the debate.

Note-Taking

Peer Evaluation

Read the assessment criteria and objectively evaluate your peers on a scale from 1 to 10.

CRITERIA	Name				
Understands the subject well	/10	/10	/10	/10	/10
Supports opinion with clear logic and examples	/10	/10	/10	/10	/10
Introduces opinions with appropriate connectors (In my view, I agree, For example, etc.)	/10	/10	/10	/10	/10
Uses a variety of vocabulary and expressions	/10	/10	/10	/10	/10
Accurately uses a variety of grammatical structures	/10	/10	/10	/10	/10
Does not monopolize the conversation and lets other people express themselves	/10	/10	/10	/10	/10
Listens attentively and respects other people's opinions	/10	/10	/10	/10	/10
Is able to accept criticism without becoming upset	/10	/10	/10	/10	/10
TOTAL SCORE	/80	/80	/80	/80	/80

Unit 04 Replacing Teachers with Computers

Organizing Ideas

Should computers replace teachers in the classroom?

Look at the reading passage in your textbook. List all the supporting arguments both FOR and AGAINST. Then, add the supporting logic and examples for each argument.

FOR	AGAINST
Argument 1	**Argument 1**
Support	**Support**
Argument 2	**Argument 2**
Support	**Support**
Argument 3	**Argument 3**
Support	**Support**

Making Supporting Examples: Expert Opinions

Expert opinions are usually the ideas and opinions of experts in any given field. Experts are typically people such as professors, doctors, and business managers. Most experts base their opinions on their years of experience doing research and working in their fields. Below are some expert opinions related to the topic of replacing teachers with computers.

Additional Research

Before starting your argument, let's do some extra research on the topic. Read the expert opinions about replacing teachers with computers.

Edward Hosteller, Education Consultant

The responsibilities of teachers go far beyond simply providing academic lessons. No doubt, teachers have teaching skills and knowledge. But even more importantly, teachers also make students feel accepted as individuals. Teachers provide positive feedback and genuine encouragement. This creates emotional bonds between teachers and students that motivate students to be more involved. Almost everybody can name at least one inspirational teacher. How can computers ever do that? Lessons delivered on computer will give students the information they need but not the attention they seek. For this reason, no computer can ever fully replace teachers.

Bridgett Newman, Educator

In today's world, teachers are unnecessary for delivering a quality education. This is supported by research conducted by the U.S. Department of Education. Researchers there found that students who took classes online performed better than students in traditional classrooms. One reason for this is the customizability of online lessons. In a traditional classroom, a teacher must create a single lesson for 30 students. Both students who have trouble understanding and students who learn quickly suffer in this situation. Online classes correct this. If students do not understand a concept, they can go back and review it as many times as they want without disturbing anyone else. In addition, fast learners can fly through lessons as quickly as they want.

Work with a partner and answer the following questions. Phrases have been provided to help you.

1. According to Edward Hosteller, what role do teachers have beyond providing academic lessons?
   → Edward Hosteller argues that teachers _____.

2. How does Edward Hosteller feel about using technology in the classroom?
   → He feels that _____.

3. How do online lessons correct the problems of having many students in a traditional classroom?
   → Online lessons make it possible to _____.

4. How could online lessons help both fast and slow learners study better?
   → They could allow fast learners to _____
   while slower learners could _____.

Your Research

Find an article about replacing teachers with computers from a magazine, newspaper, or academic website. Paste or tape the article in your workbook in the space below.

Paste or Tape Your Research Article Here

Read your article and write four specific examples or pieces of evidence you can use for your debate. Try to include different types of examples, including opinion polls, statistics, academic studies, and general facts.

- _____
- _____
- _____
- _____

Debate Note-Taking

Use this page to take notes about the opposing team's arguments during the debate.

Note-Taking

_____
_____
_____
_____
_____
_____
_____
_____
_____
_____
_____

Peer Evaluation

Read the assessment criteria and objectively evaluate your peers on a scale from 1 to 10.

CRITERIA	Name				
Understands the subject well	/10	/10	/10	/10	/10
Supports opinion with clear logic and examples	/10	/10	/10	/10	/10
Introduces opinions with appropriate connectors (In my view, I agree, For example, etc.)	/10	/10	/10	/10	/10
Uses a variety of vocabulary and expressions	/10	/10	/10	/10	/10
Accurately uses a variety of grammatical structures	/10	/10	/10	/10	/10
Does not monopolize the conversation and lets other people express themselves	/10	/10	/10	/10	/10
Listens attentively and respects other people's opinions	/10	/10	/10	/10	/10
Is able to accept criticism without becoming upset	/10	/10	/10	/10	/10
TOTAL SCORE	/80	/80	/80	/80	/80

Unit 05: Using CCTVs in Public Places

Organizing Ideas

Should governments be allowed to use CCTVs in public places?

Look at the reading passage in your textbook. List all the supporting arguments both FOR and AGAINST. Then, add the supporting logic and examples for each argument.

FOR	AGAINST
Argument 1	**Argument 1**
Support	**Support**
Argument 2	**Argument 2**
Support	**Support**
Argument 3	**Argument 3**
Support	**Support**

Making Supporting Examples: Facts

A fact is something true. For debates, you can use facts that are common knowledge, but you should also try to use more specific, less commonly known facts. The best places to find specific facts are newspaper and magazine articles. In these sources, you can find all of the details of a situation and can read interviews from people related to the story. Below are some facts related to the topic of using CCTVs in public places.

Additional Research

Before starting your argument, let's do some extra research on the topic. Read the facts about using CCTVs in public places.

CCTVs No Help in Solving Crime

New information released by London researchers suggests that the installation of CCTVs in the city has done little to help solve crimes. London has more than 10,000 cameras installed, yet nearly 80 percent of crimes go unsolved. Surprisingly, many of the neighborhoods with the highest number of CCTV cameras have the lowest crime-solving rates.

Wandsworth has 993 cameras, Tower Hamlets, 824, Greenwich, 747, and Lewisham, 730. Nevertheless, the rate of crimes solved in each of these neighborhoods is only 20 percent, which is below average for the city. In contrast, the neighborhood of Brent has only 164 cameras yet has the highest crime-solving rate in the city. 25.9 percent of crimes are solved in that neighborhood.

These figures have lawmakers calling for change. London's CCTV system cost nearly $400 million to install. A significant number of lawmakers believe it would be better to stop funding the CCTV system. Instead, they suggest increasing police patrols in all neighborhoods with high crime rates.

Defenders of CCTV systems claim that the cameras help to stop crime. They argue that the number of cameras is not as important as the placement of the cameras. Cameras must be placed so that they can easily record the faces of criminals. The cameras should also be installed in enough places so that police can track criminals before and after they commit crimes.

Work with a partner and answer the following questions. Phrases have been provided to help you.

1 How many crimes are solved in London by percentage?

→ Less than _____ are solved in the city of London.

2 What is true about the neighborhoods Wandsworth, Tower Hamlets, Greenwich, and Lewisham?

→ They have _____ , yet _____ .

3 What do some lawmakers believe the city should use instead of CCTV cameras?

→ Some lawmakers believe that the city should _____ .

4 Why is the number of cameras less important than the placement of the cameras?

→ It is less important because _____ .

Your Research

Find an article about using CCTVs in public places from a magazine, newspaper, or academic website. Paste or tape the article in your workbook in the space below.

Paste or Tape Your Research Article Here

Read your article and write four specific examples or pieces of evidence you can use for your debate. Try to include different types of examples, including opinion polls, statistics, academic studies, and general facts.

-
-
-
-

Debate Note-Taking

Use this page to take notes about the opposing team's arguments during the debate.

Note-Taking

Peer Evaluation

Read the assessment criteria and objectively evaluate your peers on a scale from 1 to 10.

CRITERIA	Name				
Understands the subject well	/10	/10	/10	/10	/10
Supports opinion with clear logic and examples	/10	/10	/10	/10	/10
Introduces opinions with appropriate connectors (In my view, I agree, For example, etc.)	/10	/10	/10	/10	/10
Uses a variety of vocabulary and expressions	/10	/10	/10	/10	/10
Accurately uses a variety of grammatical structures	/10	/10	/10	/10	/10
Does not monopolize the conversation and lets other people express themselves	/10	/10	/10	/10	/10
Listens attentively and respects other people's opinions	/10	/10	/10	/10	/10
Is able to accept criticism without becoming upset	/10	/10	/10	/10	/10
TOTAL SCORE	/80	/80	/80	/80	/80

Unit 06 Celebrity Salaries

Organizing Ideas

Should entertainers and athletes earn such high salaries?

Look at the reading passage in your textbook. List all the supporting arguments both FOR and AGAINST. Then, add the supporting logic and examples for each argument.

FOR	AGAINST
Argument 1	**Argument 1**
Support	**Support**
Argument 2	**Argument 2**
Support	**Support**
Argument 3	**Argument 3**
Support	**Support**

Making Supporting Examples: Statistics

Statistics are facts based on numbers. They are usually created by governments, universities, news organizations, and companies. Statistics often show the number of people, companies, and nations that agree with a certain opinion or policy. To show these numbers, statistics can include percentages, populations, and points. Below are some statistics related to the topic of celebrity salaries.

Additional Research

Before starting your argument, let's do some extra research on the topic. Read the statistics about celebrity salaries.

Top 10 Highest-Paying Jobs		Top 10 Highest-Paid Celebrities	
Job	Salary	Entertainer	Salary
1. Doctor	$184,650	1. Oprah Winfrey (TV host)	$165,000,000
2. Chief Executive	$176,550	2. Michael Bay (director)	$160,000,000
3. Psychiatrist	$174,170	3. Steven Speilberg (director)	$130,000,000
4. Dentist	$168,000	4. Jerry Bruckheimer (film producer)	$115,000,000
5. Petroleum Engineer	$138,980	5. Dr. Dre (music producer)	$110,000,000
6. Lawyer	$130,490	6. Tyler Perry (director)	$105,000,000
7. Marketing Manager	$126,190	7. Howard Stern (radio host)	$95,000,000
8. Airline Pilot	$118,070	8. James Patterson (author)	$94,000,000
9. Pharmacist	$112,160	9. George Lucas (director)	$90,000,000
10. Court Judge	$110,940	10. Simon Cowell (music producer)	$90,000,000

Work with a partner and answer the following questions. Phrases have been provided to help you.

1 What do most of the top 10 highest-paying jobs require in terms of education?

→ Most of the top 10 jobs require _____.

2 About how many years would a doctor have to work to earn Oprah Winfrey's yearly salary?

→ A doctor would have to work _____.

3 How is the work of the top 10 highest-paid celebrities different from that of most entertainers?

→ Their work is different because _____.

4 What is the overall message of this chart?

→ The overall message of this chart is _____.

Your Research

Find an article about celebrity salaries from a magazine, newspaper, or academic website. Paste or tape the article in your workbook in the space below.

Paste or Tape Your Research Article Here

Read your article and write four specific examples or pieces of evidence you can use for your debate. Try to include different types of examples, including opinion polls, statistics, academic studies, and general facts.

- _____
- _____
- _____
- _____

Debate Note-Taking

Use this page to take notes about the opposing team's arguments during the debate.

Note-Taking

Peer Evaluation

Read the assessment criteria and objectively evaluate your peers on a scale from 1 to 10.

CRITERIA	Name				
Understands the subject well	/10	/10	/10	/10	/10
Supports opinion with clear logic and examples	/10	/10	/10	/10	/10
Introduces opinions with appropriate connectors (In my view, I agree, For example, etc.)	/10	/10	/10	/10	/10
Uses a variety of vocabulary and expressions	/10	/10	/10	/10	/10
Accurately uses a variety of grammatical structures	/10	/10	/10	/10	/10
Does not monopolize the conversation and lets other people express themselves	/10	/10	/10	/10	/10
Listens attentively and respects other people's opinions	/10	/10	/10	/10	/10
Is able to accept criticism without becoming upset	/10	/10	/10	/10	/10
TOTAL SCORE	/80	/80	/80	/80	/80

Unit 07: Punishment for Criminals

Organizing Ideas

Should criminals be sent to prison as punishment?

Look at the reading passage in your textbook. List all the supporting arguments both FOR and AGAINST. Then, add the supporting logic and examples for each argument.

FOR	AGAINST
Argument 1	**Argument 1**
Support	**Support**
Argument 2	**Argument 2**
Support	**Support**
Argument 3	**Argument 3**
Support	**Support**

Making Supporting Examples: Expert Opinions

Expert opinions are usually the ideas and opinions of experts in any given field. Experts are typically people such as professors, doctors, and business managers. Most experts base their opinions on their years of experience doing research and working in their fields. Below are some expert opinions related to the topic of punishment for criminals.

Additional Research

Before starting your argument, let's do some extra research on the topic. Read the expert opinions about punishment for criminals.

Lewis Baca, Sheriff

The greatest danger in any society is criminals. History has shown us that the only way to make a society safer is to get criminals off the streets. The best way to do this is to put as many lawbreakers as possible into prison. Being a sheriff means I receive a lot of blame about the effectiveness of prisons. I firmly believe that prisons are effective; we just need to have enough of them. Right now, that's not the case. Almost all of our prisons are overcrowded. One of the prisons in my county is designed for 1,000 prisoners, but it currently houses over 1,500 prisoners. This creates a dangerous situation for both the prisoners and the prison guards. To make prisons work, the government must be willing to spend more money to build more prisons and to hire more prison guards.

Dr. Peter Hamilton, Criminology Professor

The Justice Department recently announced its plans to make prisoners tougher. This means no more exercise rooms, Internet, or satellite TV. This sounds like a great plan until you realize one fact: Harsh prisons do not work. If anything, creating a harsh prison environment reinforces the idea that lawbreakers are bad people. What the government must do is create programs that teach prisoners job skills and get educations. And once they're out of prison, prisoners should receive help to find jobs and housing in good neighborhoods. Prisoners do not need to be reminded that they are lawbreakers. What they need to do is learn how to be productive members of society.

Work with a partner and answer the following questions. Phrases have been provided to help you.

1 According to Lewis Baca, what is the most effective way to make society safer?

→ *Baca says the best way is to* _____.

2 What does Baca suggest governments do to make prisons more effective?

→ *He suggests that governments* _____.

3 What does Dr. Peter Hamilton believe about making prisons harsher?

→ *He believes that* _____.

4 How does Dr. Hamilton think prisoners can learn to be productive in society?

→ *Dr. Hamilton thinks* _____.

Your Research

Find an article about punishment for criminals from a magazine, newspaper, or academic website. Paste or tape the article in your workbook in the space below.

Paste or Tape Your Research Article Here

Read your article and write four specific examples or pieces of evidence you can use for your debate. Try to include different types of examples, including opinion polls, statistics, academic studies, and general facts.

- _____
- _____
- _____
- _____

Debate Note-Taking

Use this page to take notes about the opposing team's arguments during the debate.

Note-Taking

Peer Evaluation

Read the assessment criteria and objectively evaluate your peers on a scale from 1 to 10.

CRITERIA	Name				
Understands the subject well	/10	/10	/10	/10	/10
Supports opinion with clear logic and examples	/10	/10	/10	/10	/10
Introduces opinions with appropriate connectors (In my view, I agree, For example, etc.)	/10	/10	/10	/10	/10
Uses a variety of vocabulary and expressions	/10	/10	/10	/10	/10
Accurately uses a variety of grammatical structures	/10	/10	/10	/10	/10
Does not monopolize the conversation and lets other people express themselves	/10	/10	/10	/10	/10
Listens attentively and respects other people's opinions	/10	/10	/10	/10	/10
Is able to accept criticism without becoming upset	/10	/10	/10	/10	/10
TOTAL SCORE	/80	/80	/80	/80	/80

Unit 08: Cosmetic Plastic Surgery

Organizing Ideas

Should people be allowed to get plastic surgery for cosmetic purposes?

Look at the reading passage in your textbook. List all the supporting arguments both FOR and AGAINST. Then, add the supporting logic and examples for each argument.

FOR	AGAINST
Argument 1	**Argument 1**
Support	**Support**
Argument 2	**Argument 2**
Support	**Support**
Argument 3	**Argument 3**
Support	**Support**

Making Supporting Examples: Personal Experience

Personal experience is your experience related to the topic. Using personal experience can be a good way to support your argument if you explain how your experience proves your point. However, you should be careful because one person's experience might not be common. This can actually weaken your argument. Below are some personal experiences related to the topic of cosmetic surgery.

Additional Research

Before starting your argument, let's do some extra research about the topic. Read the personal experiences about cosmetic surgery.

Getting Plastic Surgery Changed My Life!

For the first time in years, Louise Harrison has a smile on her face. The 51-year-old mother of two underwent a facelift procedure at the Jewelry Plastic Surgery Center in Miami, Florida.

Before the surgery, Louis looked much older than 51. To improve her appearance, Louise had doctors perform a brow lift, a full facelift, and a neck lift. Louise explains, "The doctors were very helpful throughout the process and explained all the procedures step by step. I felt very comfortable going into the operation."

Today, Louise is a new woman. Thanks to her confidence, she got a promotion at work. "My improved appearance has made me feel more confident in myself. Getting plastic surgery changed my life!"

Medical Mistake Ends the Life of an Outgoing Mother

Sandy McCormick, mother of two, had her life cut short last week during a cosmetic surgery procedure. McCormick went last Monday for liposuction—surgery to remove fat from the waist—at the Sandy Hills Surgical Center. There, the nurse gave her an anesthetic to reduce pain. However, the nurse was not trained in giving anesthetic and ended up giving McCormick a deadly amount of the chemical. During the surgery, McCormick's heart stopped beating. She was taken to a nearby hospital where she was pronounced dead.

Danny McCormick, Sandy's husband, is still in shock. "I told Sandy that she didn't need surgery and that she looked great," he says. "She shouldn't have died because of a surgery she didn't even need."

Work with a partner and answer the following questions. Phrases have been provided to help you.

1. What is Louise Harrison's opinion of the plastic surgery process?
   → Louise's opinion is _____.

2. How has Louise's life improved because of her plastic surgery operation?
   → Her life has _____.

3. What was the cause of Sandy McCormick's death?
   → She died because _____.

4. What does Sandy's husband say about the surgery?
   → Her husband says _____.

Your Research

Find an article about cosmetic surgery from a magazine, newspaper, or academic website. Paste or tape the article in your workbook in the space below.

Paste or Tape Your Research Article Here

Read your article and write four specific examples or pieces of evidence you can use for your debate. Try to include different types of examples, including opinion polls, statistics, academic studies, and general facts.

-
-
-
-

Debate Note-Taking

Use this page to take notes about the opposing team's arguments during the debate.

Note-Taking

Peer Evaluation

Read the assessment criteria and objectively evaluate your peers on a scale from 1 to 10.

CRITERIA	Name				
Understands the subject well	/10	/10	/10	/10	/10
Supports opinion with clear logic and examples	/10	/10	/10	/10	/10
Introduces opinions with appropriate connectors (In my view, I agree, For example, etc.)	/10	/10	/10	/10	/10
Uses a variety of vocabulary and expressions	/10	/10	/10	/10	/10
Accurately uses a variety of grammatical structures	/10	/10	/10	/10	/10
Does not monopolize the conversation and lets other people express themselves	/10	/10	/10	/10	/10
Listens attentively and respects other people's opinions	/10	/10	/10	/10	/10
Is able to accept criticism without becoming upset	/10	/10	/10	/10	/10
TOTAL SCORE	/80	/80	/80	/80	/80

Unit 09: Physical Education in Schools

Organizing Ideas

Should all students be required to take physical education classes?

Look at the reading passage in your textbook. List all the supporting arguments both FOR and AGAINST. Then, add the supporting logic and examples for each argument.

FOR	AGAINST
Argument 1	**Argument 1**
Support	**Support**
Argument 2	**Argument 2**
Support	**Support**
Argument 3	**Argument 3**
Support	**Support**

Making Supporting Examples: Facts

A fact is something true. For debates, you can use facts that are common knowledge, but you should also try to use more specific, less commonly known facts. The best places to find specific facts are newspaper and magazine articles. In these sources, you can find all of the details of a situation and can read interviews from people related to the story. Below are some facts related to the topic of physical education in schools.

Additional Research

Before starting your argument, let's do some extra research on the topic. Read the facts about physical education in schools.

A Report on Childhood Exercise by the National Office of Health

It is important that schools work to provide young people as many chances as possible to become physically active. There are many benefits to physical activity, including:
- Building healthy bones and muscles
- Reducing feelings of depression and promoting mental well-being
- Improving academic performance, including grades, behavior, and concentration

On the contrary, physical inactivity presents many problems to the health of young people such as:
- An increased chance of being overweight or obese, which can lead to diabetes, high blood pressure, high cholesterol, asthma, and overall poor health
- A greater possibility of early death due to heart disease or high blood pressure

Despite these dangers, not all schools require physical activity. Our research shows:
- 77 percent of elementary school students reported getting one hour or more of physical activity weekly, while only 29 percent of high school students do so.

Requiring physical education class is the most obvious way that schools can make sure their students get enough physical exercise. Other alternatives include recess, classroom-based physical activities, and afterschool physical activity clubs.

Work with a partner and answer the following questions. Phrases have been provided to help you.

1 What are some of the health benefits of regular physical exercise?

→ Some of the health benefits are _____.

2 How can physical inactivity affect the lives of young people?

→ Inactivity can result in _____.

3 What percentage of elementary school students and high school students get regular exercise?

→ _____ of elementary school students and _____ of high school students exercise regularly.

4 What are some ways schools can encourage their students to exercise?

→ Schools can _____.

Your Research

Find an article about physical education in schools from a magazine, newspaper, or academic website. Paste or tape the article in your workbook in the space below.

Paste or Tape Your Research Article Here

Read your article and write four specific examples or pieces of evidence you can use for your debate. Try to include different types of examples, including opinion polls, statistics, academic studies, and general facts.

- _____
- _____
- _____
- _____

Debate Note-Taking

Use this page to take notes about the opposing team's arguments during the debate.

Note-Taking

_____
_____
_____
_____
_____
_____
_____
_____
_____
_____

Peer Evaluation

Read the assessment criteria and objectively evaluate your peers on a scale from 1 to 10.

CRITERIA	Name				
Understands the subject well	/10	/10	/10	/10	/10
Supports opinion with clear logic and examples	/10	/10	/10	/10	/10
Introduces opinions with appropriate connectors (In my view, I agree, For example, etc.)	/10	/10	/10	/10	/10
Uses a variety of vocabulary and expressions	/10	/10	/10	/10	/10
Accurately uses a variety of grammatical structures	/10	/10	/10	/10	/10
Does not monopolize the conversation and lets other people express themselves	/10	/10	/10	/10	/10
Listens attentively and respects other people's opinions	/10	/10	/10	/10	/10
Is able to accept criticism without becoming upset	/10	/10	/10	/10	/10
TOTAL SCORE	/80	/80	/80	/80	/80

Unit 10: Space Exploration

Organizing Ideas

Should governments spend time and money exploring outer space?

Look at the reading passage in your textbook. List all the supporting arguments both FOR and AGAINST. Then, add the supporting logic and examples for each argument.

FOR	AGAINST
Argument 1	**Argument 1**
Support	**Support**
Argument 2	**Argument 2**
Support	**Support**
Argument 3	**Argument 3**
Support	**Support**

Making Supporting Examples: Academic Studies

Academic studies are research that is done by universities, governments, and large research organizations. During these studies, researchers examine events to understand what causes them and why they are important. Using academic studies is a good way to strengthen your argument. Below are some academic studies related to the topic of space exploration.

Additional Research

Before starting your argument, let's do some extra research on the topic. Read the academic studies about space exploration.

The University of Texas – Department of Space Exploration

One of the greatest challenges facing any space program is public opinion. Only the governments of the United States, Russia, and China have enough resources to pay for space exploration programs. To see how the money spent on space programs is put to good use, consider the following:

Money Goes Back To Earth

A common complaint by the public is that the money spent on space programs is not used on Earth. Space exploration programs actually do spend money on Earth. Most notably, the money goes to pay the salaries of the scientists and astronauts involved in the program. The money is also used to pay the huge companies that build the machines used in space. A good example is the aircraft company Boeing, which built all the space shuttles that were used by NASA and develops parts of the International Space Station.

Technology Improves Our Daily Lives

Less obvious but just as important are the spinoff technologies developed because of space exploration. People's daily lives are filled with technologies made possible as a result of space exploration. The medical field has perhaps benefitted the most from space exploration. Developments include the artificial heart, which has saved the lives of more than 200 patients. New, more advanced cancer treatments are also the result of space exploration. As the space program continues, it will lead to more new technologies that make people's lives safer and more convenient.

Work with a partner and answer the following questions. Phrases have been provided to help you.

1 Which countries have been able to develop their own space exploration programs?
→ *The countries are* _____.

2 What are two ways the money spent on space exploration is used on Earth?
→ *The first way is* _____, *and the second way is* _____.

3 How do developments in the space program affect our overall technical knowledge?
→ *The developments allow* _____.

4 What are some technologies that have been developed because of the space program?
→ *Some of the technologies are* _____.

Your Research

Find an article about space exploration from a magazine, newspaper, or academic website. Paste or tape the article in your workbook in the space below.

Paste or Tape Your Research Article Here

Read your article and write four specific examples or pieces of evidence you can use for your debate. Try to include different types of examples, including opinion polls, statistics, academic studies, and general facts.

- _____
- _____
- _____
- _____

Debate Note-Taking

Use this page to take notes about the opposing team's arguments during the debate.

Note-Taking

Peer Evaluation

Read the assessment criteria and objectively evaluate your peers on a scale from 1 to 10.

CRITERIA	Name				
Understands the subject well	/10	/10	/10	/10	/10
Supports opinion with clear logic and examples	/10	/10	/10	/10	/10
Introduces opinions with appropriate connectors (In my view, I agree, For example, etc.)	/10	/10	/10	/10	/10
Uses a variety of vocabulary and expressions	/10	/10	/10	/10	/10
Accurately uses a variety of grammatical structures	/10	/10	/10	/10	/10
Does not monopolize the conversation and lets other people express themselves	/10	/10	/10	/10	/10
Listens attentively and respects other people's opinions	/10	/10	/10	/10	/10
Is able to accept criticism without becoming upset	/10	/10	/10	/10	/10
TOTAL SCORE	/80	/80	/80	/80	/80

Memo

Memo